MR. MOTHER EARTH'S
MOST REWARDING
HOUSEPLANTS

ALSO BY JOEL RAPP

Mother Earth's Vegetarian Feasts

Mother Earth's Hassle-Free Vegetable Cookbook

Dear Mother Earth

Grow with Your Plants the Mother Earth Hassle-Free Way

Mother Earth's Hassle-Free Indoor Plant Book

Mr. Mother Earth's

MOST REWARDING HOUSEPLANTS

JOEL RAPP
"Mr. Mother Earth"

Fawcett Columbine ♦ *New York*

To Susan, without whom the flowers
would smell only half as sweet.

A Fawcett Columbine Book
Published by Ballantine Books

Copyright © 1989 by Joel Rapp
Plant illustrations copyright © 1989 by Monika Bittman
Instructional illustrations copyright © 1989 by Patrick O'Brien

Library of Congress Catalog Card Number: 88-91988

ISBN: 0-449-90355-9

Interior design by Ann Gold
Cover design by James R. Harris
Cover photo by George Kerrigan

Manufactured in the United States of America
First Edition: March 1989

10 9 8 7 6 5 4 3 2 1

CONTENTS

MR. MOTHER EARTH'S
MOST REWARDING HOUSEPLANTS

INTRODUCTION

Hi there, philodendron phans!

Can you believe that it's been fifteen years since first we met in *Mother Earth's Hassle-Free Indoor Plant Book*? In those days, when we were all more or less beginning our houseplant experience, my message to you was: "I'm not a botanist or a certified horticulturist. I'm just an ordinary person who's had long and practical experience raising houseplants. After trying and failing and finally succeeding with virtually every plant that can be grown successfully indoors, I'd like to share my experience with *you*."

In those days my mission was to get you involved with plants, to help you discover, as I had, the wonders of indoor gardening and the pleasures of surrounding yourself with lush, tropical foliage.

I wanted to help you acquire, as I had, the legendary "green thumb."

Now I knew, from my own experience, that having a green thumb was only a state of mind—having confidence that plants will not only live but flourish in your home or apartment. So I urged you to buy only the simplest, easiest, most hassle-free, "impossible-to-kill" plants.

(You may remember "Mother Earth's Hassle-Free Plants": philodendron, dracaena, dieffenbachia, pothos, sanseveria, grape ivy, dwarf palm, Chinese evergreen, nephthytis, and spathiphyllum.)

Well, you did. And you've made gardening, both indoor and outdoor, America's #1 leisure time activity.

A lot of water's gone under the bridge—and into the dieffenbachias—since then, and my own plant experience has expanded beyond even *my* wildest dreams.

Raising houseplants has been my hobby—my passion, if you will—ever since I got my first plant nearly thirty years ago. It was a snake plant (*Sanseveria laurentii*), and I named it Irving. When Irving not only lived but produced new shoots—in spite of my botanical ignorance—I was hooked.

Over the years, as my addiction to houseplants grew, so did my thirst to try growing more exotic, more sophisticated, more glamorous plants. As I roamed through the nurseries and botanical gardens of the world, I found myself lusting to grow plants I'd thought were absolutely impossible without a greenhouse—

delicate ferns, beautiful flowers, showy bromeliads, remarkable bonsais. I envied the people I met who grew these plants—and even more exotic varieties—right in their living rooms, or on their kitchen windowsills.

So, I tried. I tried orchids, I nurtured African violets. I grew herbs. And, for the most part, I succeeded. And now I want to share these "most rewarding" plants with all of you. Take it from me, if you think it's fun keeping a *Ficus benjamina* alive, imagine how rewarding you'll feel succeeding with a Kafir lily or a bird's-nest fern.

I know—from the thousands of phone calls and letters I receive as a result of my television appearances, my radio programs, and my position as gardening editor at *Redbook*—that you, too, are yearning to expand your plant horizons.

Well, imagine how you'll feel when you look across the room at a windowsill of beautiful, thriving flowering plants; imagine the delight of a friend when presented with a gift of a bonsai tree you've fashioned yourself—and imagine your joy at accomplishing it; imagine training a small, inexpensive hibiscus bush into a stately standard—a plant worth over $100 and a fabulous addition to your decor as well. And these are just a few of the "most rewarding" plants that you'll encounter in these pages.

The plants you're going to come to know and love in this book have, in some cases, reputations for being temperamental. But that's only because they require a little extra time and attention—and because you've got to understand and meet their specific needs. The actual "work" involved in caring for them is minimal compared to the rewards.

So without further ado, let's begin our adventure down this most exciting garden path, the path toward success with the beauties I call "Mr. Mother Earth's Most Rewarding Houseplants"—because that's exactly what they are.

PART ONE

A Refresher Course in Houseplant Care

HOW TO GROW
A GREEN THUMB

As I've often said, having a green thumb is strictly a state of mind. Anybody can grow houseplants—absolute beginners are just as capable of growing the beautiful, exotic plants in this book as certified green-thumbers.

The key to growing your green thumb is developing confidence in your ability to get these "most rewarding" plants—plants that you're probably used to watching die—to thrive in your home or apartment.

Developing the plant-growing skills you'll need to grow Mr. Mother Earth's Most Rewarding Houseplants really isn't that difficult. You won't need to serve an internship or a residency to learn how to cultivate a coral berry or a coconut palm. All you'll need to do is learn some general guidelines for growing plants indoors, and then follow the specific care instructions for the plants that you want to try. You'll also need a little patience, a willingness to try something new, and a commitment to giving your plants the care they need.

In this section I'll give you a refresher course in the basics of indoor plant cultivation. I'll explain why some plants will grow indoors, while most won't; discuss your plant's need for proper light, water, humidity, temperature, soil, and food; and teach you the key plant-care techniques: repotting, propagation, pest control, and so on.

First, though, I'd like to talk a little about the real stars of this show—the plants.

WHAT MAKES A PLANT
"MOST REWARDING"?

Before we get started, I think it's important for you to know why I chose these particular plants from among the hundreds of "houseplants" you'll find described in plant encyclopedias.

I've used three criteria.

The first is commercial availability. You should be able to find all of the plants covered in this book in better nurseries and garden centers in any of the fifty states—including Alaska, and especially Hawaii. Not every nursery will have every plant, of course, but you're sure to come across all of them at some point.

The second criterion is even more important. Over the years I've had the opportunity to read practically every book ever written on the care of houseplants. Most of them are excellent—and accurate.

However, when it comes to giving care instructions for the various plants, I've found dozens of discrepancies. One book will suggest that you keep a certain plant moist at all times. Another will recommend that you let that same plant dry out thoroughly between waterings. One book will tell you that a plant needs lots of bright, unfiltered light; another will say that it must have shady conditions to flourish.

Now, although I'm the first to admit that houseplant care is not an exact science, I guarantee the instructions you'll find herein will work. Why? Because I've personally "kitchen tested" each and every one of "Mr. Mother Earth's Most Rewarding Houseplants."

Finally, I've chosen these particular plants because I think they're the "most rewarding"—in terms of the vitality, color, and beauty they can bring into an apartment or house—of the hundreds of different plants I've grown.

"Most rewarding" is a very subjective term. I know that many of you think that flowering plants are the most rewarding. Some people, on the other hand, absolutely adore cacti and succulents, while others can't stand their menacing look and feel. And some people will be almost as happy if they can just manage to keep a plant alive—which is why I've included several rather common and easy-to-care-for plants among my "most rewarding." Still others will only feel rewarded by trying and finally succeeding with the most challenging plants, such as ferns and orchids.

Beauty is in the eye of the beholder; one man's meat is another man's poison; there are almost as many relevant aphorisms as there are different kinds of plants. My best advice is to pick the plants you like and try them! I'm sure that you'll enjoy and appreciate them as much as I do.

How many of the plants in this book you'll be able to grow is limited only by your level of commitment. The more you learn about proper plant care, and the more involved you get with your own plants, the more successes and rewards you're bound to have.

HOW DIFFICULT WILL IT BE?

Admittedly, some of these plants will be more "difficult" to grow than others. But "difficult" is another subjective term. "More challenging" might be a better choice of words. For plant care, "difficult" simply means that many of the plants—like ferns, fittonias, and flowering plants—are going to need a bit more care than the "hassle-free" plants that got us started on the road to this new, more exciting plateau in our plant experience.

"Difficult" means that you may have to make two or three trips a week with your watering pail, instead of the single trip you're making now. It means you'll have to spray your plants every day instead of once in a while, and you'll have to make sure to remember the proper feeding schedules for your plants. If the care instructions call for "dry wells," you'll have to check the water level in the pebble tray almost daily. You'll have to be more alert to the symptoms of trouble—like yellowing leaves, drying edges, and droopy foliage—and you'll have to repot your plants once in a while.

But none of this is pick-and-shovel labor. And I think we'd all agree that nothing *really* wonderful or "most rewarding" comes without some extra care and effort.

WHAT IS AN "INDOOR" PLANT?

Simply stated, an "indoor" plant is a plant that, out of the hundreds of thousands of species and varieties that make up the plant kingdom, will adapt to living indoors in a pot; a plant that will accept the relatively constant conditions of an indoor environment, as opposed to the unfettered room for root growth and the changes of season that plants get outdoors.

Horticulturists and botanists and just plain indoor gardeners like you and me have discovered which plants can make this transition from the wild and which can't. Most of the plants that the home gardener can grow successfully are represented in this book. There are a couple of hundred more that can grow indoors, but the vast majority of them will only survive in the "indoors" of a greenhouse.

THE FAMILIES
OF PLANTS

"**M**r. Mother Earth's Most Rewarding Houseplants" fall into four basic categories:

Foliage Plants: All plants (with the exception of ferns) will flower in their native habitats, but many of the plants I've chosen are grown indoors primarily for their lush, green, sometimes strikingly patterned or colored leaves. It includes most of the common, easy-to-grow plants such as dieffenbachia, pothos, and philodendron, along with beauties like the polka-dot plant, the nerve plant, the crotons, and the coleus. It includes virtually all plants whose flowers are less than a couple of inches in diameter—but you'll probably never see these flowers while you've got the plant in your house or apartment. Still, these plants are tremendously rewarding—not only because they're beautiful, but also because they're the most useful plants for decorating your home.

Cacti and Succulents: Because their native habitats are usually deserts, these are tremendously hardy plants. They've adapted, over the centuries, to deal with extreme conditions of heat, cold, and drought. Cacti and succulents store water in their leaves and stems. As a result, they are particularly easy to care for, as long as you provide them with lots of good bright sun and don't overwater them.

In many instances, with a little extra effort—making sure that your cactus plants experience long and cool nights during the winter—your plant can further reward you by blooming. The legendary cactus flowers are delicate and beautiful, and look quite incongruous on their spiny, menacing hosts.

Bromeliads: There are almost two thousand species in this large and fascinating family—which includes various varieties of *Aechmea*, *Vriesia*, *Guzmania*, *Tillandsia*, *Cryptanthus*, and others. The one you're probably most familiar with is the pineapple plant *(Ananus)*.

Most bromeliads are very exotic in appearance—somewhere between a cactus and a foliage plant—and almost all are epiphytes. An epiphyte is a plant that attaches itself to a host and then takes its nourishment directly from the air. (Unlike a parasite, which actually lives off its host.)

In your house or apartment, however, you'll have to provide your bromeliads with food and water. Bromeliads should, as a general rule, be watered in their "cups," or in the centers of the "rosettes" most varieties form. (Spanish moss is one exception to this rule—all you have to do is mist it!)

Indoors, all bromeliads should be misted daily. You should add a little water-soluble plant food to the misting water about once a month. I recommend regular houseplant food, but for what it's worth, the greatest collection of bromeliads I've ever seen was tended by an amateur gardening friend of mine who fed *his* bromeliads by spraying them with 7-Up!

Flowering Plants: Many people consider these plants—grown for the flowers they produce—to be the most rewarding plants of all.

I certainly remember the thrill I got the first time I coaxed an African violet into bloom. It was like becoming a father! And every time an orchid plant blooms anew, or a "dead" cyclamen or gloxinia or amaryllis returns, I get goose bumps.

You'll find that flowering plants are generally more challenging than the foliage plants, the cacti and succulents, or the bromeliads. If you're going to try any of these beautiful plants, be prepared for a few disappointments. If they're listed among "Mr. Mother Earth's Most Rewarding Houseplants," though, you can rest assured that with patience and perseverance you, too, can feel the thrill of nurturing a blossom into the world.

CHOOSING THE
RIGHT PLANT FOR YOU

The first and perhaps the most important step on your trip down the indoor garden path is buying the proper plants for *you*: plants that suit your tastes, the environment in which you live, and your particular life-style.

There are several ways to choose the right plant, or plants, to buy.

You may be looking for a plant to fit in a specific location: a tree for that bare corner; a hanging plant to clock an unsightly view; a plant that flowers to liven up your windowsill. If this is your highest priority, check the lists in the back of the book for plants that fit specific environments—for example, for "Trees," for "Plants for the Shade," for "Flowering Plants," and so on.

Next, look through the individual entries for the plants you've found in the lists to see which of the candidates you find most attractive. Then read the recipes, or profiles, to see whether you'll be able to provide the proper conditions for that plant to thrive.

For example, let's say that you're looking for an indoor tree to fill up that aforementioned bare corner. Leaf through the plant recipes, looking for a tree that appeals to you. Let's say that the camellia catches your eye. Wow! What a gorgeous plant!

But wait. . . . Do you really have enough light in that corner for a camellia? When you read the care instructions, you'll note that the camellia needs bright light—specifically, western or southern sunlight. Unfortunately, your corner only gets the equivalent of northern or filtered eastern light at best.

Okay, so the camellia wasn't such a great choice. It's not the end of the world. Keep looking until you find another tree that *will* be right at home in that particular location. Check out the kentia palm, for instance. Or even the fiddle-leaf fig.

You'll come to love the tree you eventually choose, especially because it will thrive in your corner—and won't give you the headaches that the wrong plant can. Once you've got that bare corner covered, you might even be able to find another spot that's bright enough for a small camellia.

Or maybe, rather than searching for a plant for a specific location, you're just looking for a plant to add to your collection, or one that will reward you with flowers, or beautifully colored foliage, or whatever.

No matter which of these reasons motivates you, you'll have to ask yourself whether you'll be able to give the plant the proper care.

First, do you have enough sunlight to successfully raise this plant? Lack of proper light is *the* most common limiting factor, because you can usually control the other important care factors—water, humidity, temperature, and food.

As you'll see in the section on light that follows, you can, in some cases, replace natural sunlight with artificial light. Unfortunately, this isn't always practical. So be absolutely sure you can give the plant that strikes your fancy the proper light.

Next, do you go out of town on weekends, or do you travel a lot on business? If so, you're probably going to have problems with the more exotic of my "Most Rewarding Houseplants." These plants require attention and effort. If you're away frequently, you won't have time to give your plants the care they need. The plants will suffer, and you won't reap the rewards.

(If you only go away a couple of times a year—on vacation or on business—the section titled "Vacation Care" will show you how to take care of your plants.)

The bottom line: Frequent flyers should stick to low-maintenance, hassle-free plants like philodendron, arrowhead, or Chinese evergreen.

Another important consideration: Some plants—like fuschia, dwarf citrus, and geraniums, for example—really need a couple of months outside (in the shade) during the late spring and summer to do their very best. If you live in an apartment or a house where you can't give them an outdoor vacation sheltered from the sun and rain, you should avoid those plants and move on to a coffee plant, a Norfolk Island or "star" pine, or some other plant that doesn't require an outside vacation.

Developing a good idea of the kinds of plants you want—and that fit your needs—will help you make sure you're choosing the right plant. Before you head for the plant shop or garden center, check the tables in the back of the book and flip through the recipes and illustrations to put together a list of plants that you can call "Plants for Me."

SHOPPING FOR PLANTS

You'll find houseplants for sale everywhere: supermarkets, street corners, garage sales, flea markets, the backs of vans—you name it. I've seen lots of terrific plants for sale in these kinds of places—but I've also seen quite a few that were on their last legs (or is that "last leaves"?). Unless you're an expert at detecting diseased or failing plants, you're better off buying your plants at a plant shop, nursery, or garden center.

How can you tell if a plant is healthy? Give the plant a close examination before you buy it. The foliage should be bushy, shiny, and lustrous, and it should have the maximum foliage for its species because there's sure to be some leaf drop when you bring it home. The plant should be free of brown or yellow spots, and there should be few, if any, brown tips on the ends of the leaves. Most important, it should be free of pests. Look carefully for any signs of mealybugs, mites, aphids, and other insects. (See "Pests.")

One of the problems you'll have buying plants outside of plant stores or garden centers is that there's no way you can be sure that a plant hasn't been exposed to extremes of heat or cold, which will weaken its root system and diminish its chances of surviving in your house or apartment. And you can't tell if it's been tended properly while awaiting sale—and, if it fails, you probably won't get any satisfaction.

The plants on sale at reputable plant purveyors have been shipped directly from a reputable grower and most surely will have been properly cared for while waiting for someone to buy them and take them home. And if you develop a relationship with your plant salesperson, he or she will almost always "make good" on the occasional plant that fails within a week to ten days after purchase.

(Yes, this does happen. Sometimes, despite everybody's precautions—from the grower to the plant store to you—a plant will simply expire when brought into a given house or apartment. You have not committed planticide and should not be saddled with either the guilt or the financial loss.)

How to choose a plant shop or garden center? If the establishment has been in business for more than two years, if the staff can answer specific questions about the care for specific plants (you can check their answers against this book), you can probably assume that you're in good hands.

As far as selection goes, a big part of the reward of growing some of these plants will be finding them! Your average florist, garden center, plant store, or nursery will always have a large selection of "staples"—plants like pothos, spathiphyllum, perhaps an African violet or two. But if you're looking for exotic and unusual plants—like bromeliads, a snow rose, a panda plant—you're probably going to have to track down the nurseries where these more unusual plants are grown.

One good approach is to call first and ask about specific plants. On the other hand, nothing is more fun for a plant lover than taking a day to travel from nursery to nursery—searching for that perfect specimen or a really rare plant. I still clearly remember the day I found, in the little town of New Hope, Pennsylvania, the most beautiful Irish lace fern that I've ever seen.

Your plant store or garden center will also have the plant supplies you're going to need to cultivate your new plants: terra-cotta pots (see "Transplanting"), potting mix (see "Soil"), grow-lights, plant food, saucers, pebbles, spray bottles (see "Humidity"), sphagnum moss, osmunda or fir bark (if the plant you're buying requires them—see "Potting Mixes"), and insecticidal soap.

Try to buy everything you'll need while you're at the store. If your plants are suddenly attacked by mealybugs or whiteflies, for example, you'll be able to nip them in the bud if you've got some insecticidal soap on hand. And how many times have you let a plant that needed repotting sit around for weeks, even months, because you didn't have time to get back to the plant store? The Plant Scout motto is: *Be Prepared.* You won't get merit badges, but you will get greater rewards from your plants.

Now let's get growing!

CARING FOR
YOUR PLANTS

It may sound weird, but one of the most important things you can do to help your plants grow is to be personally involved with them. Plants are, after all, living things.

It's been written that music soothes the savage breast. It's also been proven scientifically that it helps plants to grow. Your attention, the sound of music, and the sound of your gentle voice will help stimulate their growth and generally keep them happier and healthier.

A raft of sophisticated scientific evidence supports these claims, but the best experiment I've seen was performed by a botanist at a major West Coast college. He put three sets of identical plants into three separate rooms—with identical growing conditions. In the first room he played only rock music—and the plants thrived. In the second room he played only classical music—and the plants thrived. In the third room he played only the news—and those plants all died!

I believe! I love my plants and they grow. I talk to them—and I'm sure they hear me. Plants are dumb; they don't have vocal cords, and they don't reason. But they *can* respond.

If you treat your plants right—both by giving them the proper care and, especially, by *caring* for them—you'll *see* their dramatic response in their green and healthy growth. Sure, it's a miracle—but it's a miracle that we're all here in the first place.

With that in mind, let's move on to the basic guidelines for maintaining the lushest, greenest plant-tation on your block.

LIGHT

All houseplants need light, but very few require direct sunlight. As a general rule, most plants will do just fine with average light—which corresponds to a standard eastern exposure. This will provide the plant with direct morning sun and indirect, fairly bright light for the remainder of the day.

Some plants need less light than others—for example, *Aspidistra,* Chinese evergreen, *Neanthe bella* palm, philodendron, spathiphyllum, and many others will do just fine with only a northern exposure, which will give them indirect light all day long.

Others need bright light: all flowering plants, cacti and succulents, and plants with brightly colored leaves, such as crotons or coleus, will do best in the bright light of a western or southern window. This is the most intense light and will provide bright sunlight for several hours each day.

You'll notice that I prescribe "filtered" light throughout the plant recipes. This refers to light that's coming in through light shades or curtains.

If your plant is not getting enough light it will droop, some of the leaves will turn yellow, it will fail to grow, and it will not produce its expected blooms. If it's getting too much light the color of its leaves will fade and lose their luster, and it will eventually burn up.

Rotate your plants regularly. If each side gets equal exposure to the source of light the plant will grow more evenly.

If you don't have enough natural light to grow houseplants, don't despair. Fluorescent lights work wonders for most plants, as do the lights specially designed for growing plants. Even incandescent light will stimulate growth as long as the plant is kept far enough away from the light source so that it's not burned by the heat.

I cannot stress enough the importance of giving your plants the proper light. Remember, the only plant that will grow in the dark is the mushroom.

WATERING

All plants need water to live; but you should keep in mind that *more plants die from overwatering than from any other cause.*

How does this happen? A plant's root system is its "heart," sending water and nourishment to its leaves and stems, causing it to grow. In the wild, where the root system has lots of room to grow and expand, it can take on an almost unlimited amount of water. The plant, in turn, can grow and grow until it reaches the maximum height for its species.

That's why you'll find philodendrons growing fifty to sixty feet tall in the rain forests of South America. In captivity, however, that same philodendron's root system has to grow in a limited space, let's say a pot that's only six inches in diameter. Once the roots fill the pot they can only accommodate a limited amount of water. Any more water and the stems, leaves and roots will become waterlogged and begin to rot.

So please adhere to the following rule: *Never water your plants until the soil is dry to the touch.*

Like all good rules, this one has exceptions: Certain plants, like cacti and succulents, store water in their leaves, and need very little watering. Others, like flowering plants and ferns, need to be watered more frequently, *before* their soil dries out.

Too much water can cause root rot and certain death. Not enough water and the plant will dry up. How to tell when to water? The solution is simple: Feel the soil with your finger—at a depth of about an inch below the surface, or down to your first knuckle. If that soil is dry, water. If it's still moist, wait a couple of days. *(Ill. 1)*

If brown and yellow spots have begun to appear on the leaves, and the plant is getting mushy, stop watering! If the plant has really been soaked, you should unpot it, remove most of the overwatered soil, and then repot it in fresh, dry soil.

There are a few other points to remember about watering. Always water thoroughly: until water comes out of the hole at the bottom of the pot. Small plants in small pots need to be watered more frequently than large plants in larger pots. Plants in plastic containers need less water than those in terra-cotta pots. Plastic

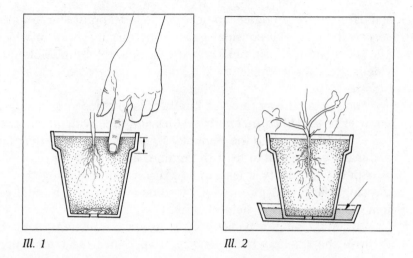

Ill. 1   Ill. 2

keeps in water longer than clay, which is porous and "breathes"—allowing more water to evaporate. Plants in bright, sunny windows will dry out more quickly than those in shadier spots.

As a general rule, add water directly to the soil that surrounds the plant. Most bromeliads, though, should be watered in their cups—or "rosettes." I recommend watering some plants—like the African violet—from below. Where I've specified this method, sit the plant—in its clay pot—in a saucer filled with a couple of inches of water. Remove it when all of the water has been sucked up by the plant's roots. *(Ill. 2)*

And remember that most of the plants in this book go through seasonal changes that affect their need for watering. Most go dormant during the fall and winter months and will require less, little, or no watering during that period (see "Seasonal Adjustments").

Be a cautious waterer—don't overdo it. And don't rely on any of the commercially available watering meters. Use your fingers to test the soil. Have a physical relationship with your plants—you'll both appreciate it.

HUMIDITY

Plants thrive on the proper level of humidity—and giving them the humidity they need is one key to raising "Mr. Mother Earth's Most Rewarding Houseplants." Remember, most of these plants grow wild in tropical climates, where the humidity can range from 70 to 90 percent. The closer you can come to approximating their natural habitats, the better they'll grow. Dry heat (in winter) and air-conditioning (in summer) can bring the humidity in a room down as low as 20 to 30 percent—and both can be major plant killers.

You can fight low humidity in a number of ways. The best way is to get a standard room humidifier. You can buy a good humidifier for under thirty dollars, so you should really consider getting one for any room in which you—and your plants—spend lots of time. The extra humidity the noiseless little machines provide is great for your plants, and good for you, too, especially during the winter months.

Another good way to boost humidity is to place your plants on a "dry well"— a saucer or tray filled first with pebbles and then with water. The water will evaporate *upward* and keep the humidity level higher around the plant. You'll have to add water to the well at least three times a week. *(Ill. 3)*

Spray your plants at least once a day. Group them together if it's aesthetically pleasing. Plants transpire, giving off some of their own humidity, so keeping them in a group can be very helpful.

During the summer, take your more temperamental plants outside and place them in the shade, where they can experience ideal humidity for a couple of months. They may have a little trouble readjusting when you bring them back indoors, but they'll manage, and, just like people, they'll benefit from the vacation. Just make sure that they're free of pests when you bring them back in.

FEEDING

Plants have to eat, but only in moderation. Because houseplants will eventually use up the nutrients in their soil, you'll have to add new nutrients from time to time.

Plant foods come in tablet, stick, powder, and liquid forms. I prefer either powdered or liquid water-soluble foods. Another fertilizer, pure fish emulsion, is

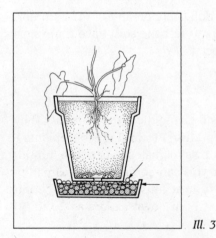

Ill. 3

also very good for your plants, but it's most odoriferous, and your plants will be just as happy with an odorless food.

Almost any commercial houseplant food will work—although I prefer Miracle-Gro. If you're growing flowering plants, use one of the foods designed for their special needs.

The nutrients included in the plant food are indicated by the three-number formula on the label—Miracle-Gro, for instance, has an 8–7–6 formulation. These numbers stand for the ratio of nitrogen, phosphorus, and potash in the food. (The middle number of the formulation should be higher for a flowering plant's food.)

All three ingredients are great for your houseplants: The nitrogen stimulates leaf growth, the phosphoric acid (or phosphates) help the plant put down roots, and the potash (or potassium) helps the plant to bloom.

I recommend feeding your foliage plants once every two weeks—following the directions on the package—*during the spring and summer only*. The package may suggest more frequent feedings, such as with every watering, but that's just a way to sell more plant food. Feed your flowering plants *every week* during the same period. During the winter months most plants go dormant, or at least slow down their rate of growth—and don't really need feeding.

I'm often asked about the value of feeding coffee grounds, tea leaves, eggshells, or any number of other "people foods" to your plants. My answer is to stick with the commercial houseplant foods. Yes, some acid-loving plants, such as hibiscus or pteris fern, might benefit from a dose of coffee or tea, but most others will suffer. And yes, some plants could conceivably find some benefit from the calcium in eggshells, but I can't imagine which ones or why. Better to be safe than sorry. Feed the table scraps to your dog.

Finally, if you have plants you don't really want to grow much bigger—if you want them to stay the same size for decorative reasons, or because you don't have enough room—then feed them only once during the growing season. Or, better yet, don't feed them at all. Just be sure to re-pot them in fresh soil at least once every few years to replenish their supply of depleted nutrients.

SEASONAL ADJUSTMENTS

Most indoor plants, especially flowering plants, feel the effects of the seasons—although their seasons are not as pronounced as those of their outdoor brothers and sisters.

During the spring and summer your plants will be getting lots of sun and a good deal more humidity—although air-conditioning can steal great gobs of humidity. Your plants will be growing the most—and you should be tending them most carefully—during these months.

Winter brings shorter days, less sunlight, dry heat, and cold drafts, none of which are particularly good for your plants. Fortunately, while you should do what you can to keep your plants healthy during the winter—by protecting them from extremes of heat, cold, or humidity—plants also help themselves by going into hibernation, or dormancy.

There are various degrees of dormancy. Plants that grow from bulbs, tubers, or rhizomes—such as amaryllis, cyclamen, gloxinia, and caladium—go completely dormant. Their foliage will die back, and you'll see no growth for as long as several months (depending on the particular variety of plant). During that time, store these plants, which will appear to be no more than dirt-filled pots, in a cool, dry place, such as a closet or basement, and stop all watering and feeding. When their spring growing season arrives (and please don't forget about the plants you've put away!) bring them out into the light and resume their regular feeding and watering.

Most of the plants—the fibrous rooted plants—don't go completely dormant. Instead, they "rest" during the late fall and winter, because there's usually a great deal less sunshine and humidity. You'll see some new growth on the more hardy specimens, but for the most part you're better off letting them sleep. Cut way back on your watering during these gray, dreary days—water your plants only after they've dried out completely, and stop feeding altogether until the growth season—spring and summer—returns.

POTTING MIXES

Since overwatering is such a danger to your indoor plants, it's important that they be potted in a light, airy, sterilized potting mix or soil. Unless I recommend a special soil in the plant profile, any of the dozens of brands of commercial potting mixes available will work just fine.

Buy a potting mix made out of loam, perlite, and peat moss. "Soil-less" mixes, which contain perlite, peat moss, vermiculite, and plant nutrients, are just as good, but don't absorb water quite as well.

It's a whole lot easier to buy a bag of potting mix than to make your own. Homemade potting mix is made up of one-third garden loam, one-third peat moss, and one-third perlite. This mixture gets baked in a 450-degree oven for a couple of hours. The baking sterilizes the soil, but it will also stink up your house or apartment.

Dirt from the garden is a no-no in houseplant culture. The pure, claylike loam is much too dense to accommodate houseplants, whose roots need lots of air.

Some of "Mr. Mother Earth's Most Rewarding Houseplants" need special soil mixtures. For example, cacti and succulents prefer a more sandy soil, and orchids and other flowering plants are best grown in osmunda or fir bark, which provide greater drainage.

GROOMING AND PRUNING

Keep the foliage of your leafy plants dust-free with regular spraying and an occasional bath with soap and water (one part soap to ten parts water).

Pruning, or cutting back your plants, is vital to keeping them looking their best. Although every plant benefits from an occasional pruning—the process encourages new and bushier growth—some plants need haircuts more frequently than others.

Because ferns, Swedish ivy, wandering Jew—all the vining varieties—are usually hung where the humidity is at its lowest (heat rises, reducing the humidity for hanging plants), they will frequently dry up. These plants should be cut back as soon as they begin to turn brown and straggly.

Simply take the plant from its hanger or shelftop, go outside or to the garbage pail, and cut off all the dead and dying foliage. Then water it thoroughly, place it in a bright, sunny place indoors, or in a shady spot outdoors in spring or summer, and it will burgeon forth anew, year in and year out.

PESTS

Although, as I've said, human error kills more plants than anything else, pests can also take their toll. Mealybugs, scale, aphids, whiteflies, thrips, and red spider mites are among the most common of the "critters" that can attack houseplants.

An ounce of prevention—keeping your plants clean, using sterilized potting soil, and checking plants carefully for pests before you buy them—is usually worth a pound of cure.

Sometimes, unfortunately, it isn't worth tuppence. Some of these microscopic creatures are hard to detect or eliminate, and sometimes a plant will be attacked in spite of all our precautions.

Mealybugs will look like tiny white cotton balls; scale will appear as tiny, oval, brown, shiny objects on the stems and undersides of leaves; and red spider mites will look like a rusty dust on the undersides of leaves. The rest will be visible as live, active "bugs."

The first thing to do when you notice pests is to separate the affected plant from your other plants. Take it into a separate part of the house to treat it, so that the problem doesn't spread to your healthy plants.

Fortunately, it's no longer necessary to attack individual mealybugs with cotton swabs dipped in alcohol, or to use foul-smelling and highly toxic insecticides or systemic poisons like malathion that go directly into the soil and root systems.

The advent of insecticidal soaps has made dealing with pests much simpler. Several brands are available, and all are equally effective, although I prefer Safer. Just a few applications of insecticidal soap should rid the plant of its problem.

If the soap treatment doesn't work, then you're better off discarding the plant. It may be painful, especially if you've become attached to that particular specimen, but you don't want to run the risk of the pests spreading to your other plants. Remember, the hurt won't last forever. There are plenty of other "Mr. Mother Earth's Most Rewarding Houseplants" left for you to try your hand at.

TRANSPLANTING

One of the most feared, yet one of the easiest, operations of indoor gardening is the common transplant.

Repotting, or transplanting, becomes necessary when your plant is root-bound and just sits there, failing to grow. The best indication that a plant needs to be repotted is the sight of roots coming through the drainage hole at the bottom of the pot. Another sign that your plant is rootbound is if water rushes through and out the bottom when you water.

There's no need to call a tree surgeon for this simple task. Just remember a few basic rules and, in most cases, your plant will come through the operation as good as new; better, in fact, since the object of the transplant is to give the roots new freedom to grow.

Transplanting is an easy, seven-step operation:

1. First, get a large pot, not less than two inches or more than four inches in diameter larger than the plant's old home. Make sure that the new pot is made out of terra-cotta (red clay). I prefer terra-cotta over plastic because it's more porous, which both permits more air to get to the roots and helps prevent overwatering.
2. Place a clay pot chip over the drainage hole in the new pot, so that water and soil won't run out too quickly.
3. Add fresh, commercial potting mix into the new pot until it's about one-third full.
4. Take the plant out of the old pot and gently loosen the soil around the roots, removing some of the old soil. Work quickly and gently, so that the plant will not suffer from damage or trauma. *(Ill. 4)*
5. Place the plant into its new container, adding or subtracting fresh soil *below* the plant until it's at a desirable, decorative height. *(Ill. 5)*
6. Now start adding soil *around* the plant, packing it down tightly until the soil is level, and about one-half inch below, the top of the pot.
7. Water the newly potted plant thoroughly, and put it in a shady spot for a day or two to let its roots establish contact with their new environment.

In a few short months your plant will have grown tremendously.

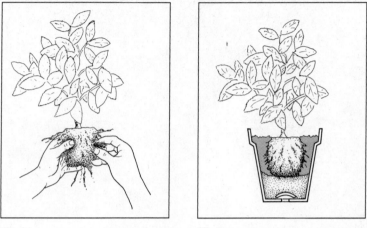

Ill. 4   Ill. 5

PROPAGATING

Making new plants from old, or sex in the greenhouse. Call it what you will, propagating your own plants is easy, fun, and very rewarding. (You'll find the correct method for each plant listed in the plant's recipe.)

There are five basic ways to propagate houseplants:

Seeds: Hardly anyone raises houseplants from seeds, but if you want to try to grow new plants from the seeds produced by your existing plants, nothing could be easier.

Simply fill a tray or traylike container with some rooting mixture—commercially available vermiculite is best—and dampen it. Sow the seeds about half an inch deep and an inch apart. Keep the tray in a bright, warm location and seedlings should soon appear. Separate the larger, stronger seedlings and put them into two-inch-diameter pots with a mixture of half potting mix and half peat moss. Cover each pot with a plastic baggie, and keep them in a bright, warm spot, watering daily, for about two weeks. At that point you can remove the plastic "greenhouse" and let the plantlets grow on their own.

Stem Cuttings: Stem cuttings can be taken from most of the plants in this book. Simply cut a piece of stem from the plant, right above a leaf node, using sharp scissors or a razor blade. Plant the stem either in damp vermiculite or directly into water. *(Ill. 6)*

The advantage of using vermiculite (which must be kept damp at all times) is that the root system will be stronger than one that forms in water. Rooting your cuttings in water is more fun, though, because you can actually see the roots forming and growing.

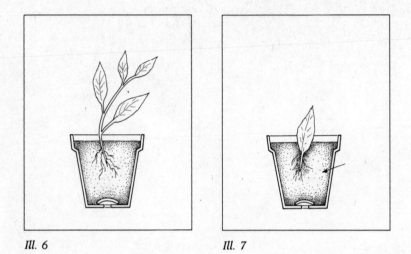

Ill. 6   Ill. 7

In the case of plants like pothos, philodendron, nephthytis, Chinese evergreen, dracaena, and many more, the cuttings can be kept growing in water alone for up to and sometimes more than a year.

Leaf Cuttings: This method is similar to using stem cuttings, but only a leaf and about half an inch of stem should be used. Submerge the stem and the bottom third of the leaf in damp vermiculite. *(Ill. 7)* New plantlets should appear in two to four weeks. African violets are the most familiar plant that can be propagated from leaf cuttings.

Division: This process is the best for bromeliads and various succulents. To divide a plant into two or more, simply cut through the root system with a very sharp knife *(Ill. 8)*, then repot the sections into individual pots with fresh potting mix and six drops of a vitamin B_1 solution. (This helps ward off shock.)

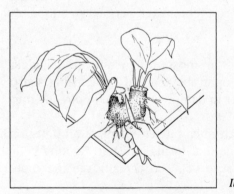

Ill. 8

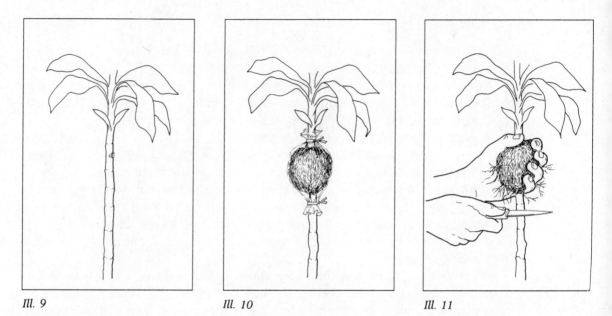

Ill. 9   *Ill. 10*   *Ill. 11*

Air-layering: This technique is a bit more complicated. It's used on woody or thick-stemmed plants like yuccas and dieffenbachias. If your dieffenbachia, for instance, has grown tall and leggy and you'd like to make two plants (or more) out of one, then air-layering is a good bet.

Pick a spot as far down or as near to the top of the plant as is aesthetically pleasing to you—but below the lowest leaves or leaf buds. This will be the base of your new plant.

Then, using a razor blade, cut a notch in the side of the trunk. Place a small piece of toothpick into the notch to keep it open *(Ill. 9)*, and wrap damp sphagnum moss around the notch, securing it in place with a plastic baggie or some plastic wrap. *(Ill. 10)*

Every two or three days, remove the plastic, spray the moss with your mister, and then put the plastic back on. Within three weeks roots will have grown out from the notch in the trunk.

Now cut through the trunk about an inch below the rooted notch. *(Ill. 11)* Plant the part of the plant that you've removed in a six-inch-diameter pot filled with fresh potting mix. The remaining stem can be cultivated as before—keeping the plant in a bright spot and watering it enough to keep the soil damp. Soon, two little shoots will emerge from either side of the stem and eventually form a new plant.

If the stem, or cane, that remains is too long, it can be cut up into six-inch-long pieces that can be individually rooted in vermiculite or water.

VACATION CARE

One of the questions I'm asked most often is "What can I do about my plants when I go on vacation?"

There's no point in going on vacation if you're going to spend it worrying about what's happening at home. I've known plant lovers who take their prize specimens with them (just to be safe), but I think that's extreme.

A great deal depends on how long you plan to be away. If you're only going for a week or less, you shouldn't have any problems. Simply water each and every one of your plants thoroughly, remove them from the windowsills, and group them together where they're not directly exposed to the sun. When you return they'll be barely the worse for wear. They may have a brown tip here, a drooping leaf there, perhaps, but all in all your plants should perk right up when they hear your key in the lock—and then get that welcome-home drink of water and an invigorating spray.

If you're going to be gone for more than a week, however, you'll have to take more elaborate steps. Since there's no such thing (yet) as a kennel for boarding houseplants, the ideal solution is to find a friend or neighbor with whom you can trust your key and your plants, and to ask that person to drop in at least once a week while you'll be out of town. (Twice a week would be better yet, especially during the summer, when plants may overheat.)

If you can't find a friend or neighbor to help out, your next move should be to check your local Yellow Pages, where you're sure to find a licensed and bonded professional plant maintenance service that will send someone to care for your plants while you're away.

If you can't find a friend and can't afford a professional plant service, there are still ways to protect your plants and make sure that they'll be in reasonably good shape on your return.

First, remove all of your plants from windowsills, shelves, and tabletops and group them together, preferably in the center of a room. Plants in groups offer each other humidity, not to mention companionship.

During the late spring or summer, a screened-in porch would be ideal for this purpose. Otherwise, a relatively airy room with enough windows to provide some indirect light is fine. If there's not enough light from natural sources, augment the light with a standing lamp with at least a 150-watt bulb.

Water all of the plants thoroughly. To make sure that your plants get enough humidity, place each plant on a saucer or tray filled with pebbles (also known as a *dry well*) and then fill the tray with water.

Place as many thoroughly watered plants as you can into a large, clear plastic bag—available from any dry cleaner—and tie the bag shut. (You may want to use stakes to support the plastic.) Use as many bags as necessary to hold all of your plants. This creates a miniature greenhouse and should keep the plants thriving for four to six weeks.

To create an even more elaborate greenhouse, you can use your bathtub, some empty pots, and several large plastic bags. First, close the drain and put about six inches of water into the tub. Then, take an empty terra-cotta pot (one for each plant) and set it upside-down in the water. Now, take your potted plants and set them atop the inverted pots. Tape the plastic bags together, and tape one end of the joined bags to the bathroom wall, the other end to the side of the tub. Leave a light on in the bathroom and this homemade greenhouse will keep your plants fresh for at least six weeks—maybe longer. *(Ill. 12)*

If some of your plants are real water lovers, like ferns, spathiphyllum, or any of the flowering plants, here's an easy method of keeping them moist during your absence: You can construct a watering device from a container of water and some sort of wick, such as a heavy shoelace or a thin piece of rope.

Fill a container with water and immerse half of the wick. Set the container next to the plant and place the other half of the wick on the top of the soil. Through a process called capillary action water will crawl up the wick as long as there is water in the container. And, as long as the wick stays wet, the soil will receive constant new moisture. *(Ill. 13)*

Three or four wicks can be used in one container to water more than one plant at a time. It's best to cover the top of the container and thread the wicks through holes punched or cut in the top—this stops water loss through evaporation.

Follow all the tips I've given you and your plants will survive your absence without too many problems.

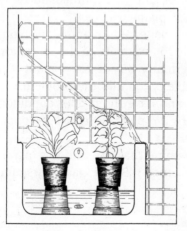

Ill. 12   *Ill. 13*

If you just can't leave your plants home alone, you can always buy a couple of dozen new ones, gather them all together in your living room, and spend a week fantasizing that you're vacationing on a tropical island.

FINE-TUNING YOUR CARE

Between the basic care techniques we've covered and the specific information in the plant profiles, you have a complete recipe for success for every plant in this book.

However, it's important that you realize that each plant has its own personality, that every plant-growing environment makes its own special demands, and that every plant grower (that's you) has his or her own personal style when it comes to plant care.

It's taken me years of trial and error to arrive at the plant care recipes—and to check them out so that I'm confident that they're accurate.

But just as you learn, through trial and error, to fiddle with recipes when you cook—adding a pinch more of this, a pinch less of that, or changing baking times to suit your oven—you're going to have to learn to fiddle with the care instructions—again, through trial and error—to succeed with *your* plants.

For example: Even if you follow all of my recommendations for caring for an African violet to the letter, your plant may still fail to produce blooms. You may have to move it to a spot where it gets more sunlight, or perhaps feed it more. If you notice that the stems are starting to get mushy, you'll have to try watering it a bit less than I advise. If the edges of the leaves begin to turn brown and brittle, you'll have to try spraying it a bit more than I've recommended.

If you pay attention to the signals the plant sends, such as drooping leaves ("I need water!") or yellowing leaves ("I'm hungry!"), and take immediate remedial action, you will almost always succeed with your plants.

Note that I said "almost always." These are challenging plants—and you will have failures. A particular plant may not be able to acclimate to the conditions in your house or apartment. Or you may inadvertently buy a weak plant. Unless you're a plant expert, you probably won't be able to identify the problem.

If you really love a particular kind of plant and have the proper conditions in which to grow it, trust in Mr. Mother Earth: Try the plant at least a second, and preferably a third time (depending on the cost).

If you don't get it right by your third try, assume that you and that particular kind of plant simply aren't meant for each other. "Smart gardeners, foolish choices"—or something like that.

PART TWO

The Stars
of the Show

HOW TO USE
THE PLANT PROFILES

Well, here they are. The stars of the show. The real raison d'être for this book: "Mr. Mother Earth's Most Rewarding Houseplants."

But first a few words on how to use the recipes, or plant profiles.

Please take the time to read the entries. They provide both the basic and key elements of care—for light, water, humidity, and temperature*—for each plant, along with solutions for some of the most commonly encountered problems.

As far as proper food and soil are concerned, follow the general rules in this section *unless otherwise noted* in the recipe.

For example, use sterilized, commercial potting mix *unless* you're going to grow orchids or *Aphelandra*. The recipes for those two plants recommend that you use fir bark instead. Feed all of your plants with Miracle-Gro or other commercial houseplant food, except for the flowering plants—which should be fed with a flowering plant food.

I've also included a few hopefully entertaining and educational anecdotes about my own experiences with the plants. I promise that reading the recipes will be practically painless, and will be a very valuable help to your chances of success and the rewards you'll get from growing these plants.

Start with my instructions and make your own trial and error adjustments, and you'll quickly discover exactly the right program of care for your plants under your unique conditions.

Happy growing!

---

*For a quick reference, look for the care symbols. These will give you a general idea of the needs of each plant on a scale of one to four: ❋ —light;   ◨—water;   ◖ —humidity;   ▯ —temperature.

African Violet

SAINTPAULIA IONANTHA
and its cultivars and hybrids

The African violet is America's most popular—and often its most frustrating—houseplant. How many times have you bought an African violet in full, glorious bloom, watched the blooms die, and then waited months, even years—gnashing your teeth because no new blooms appeared?

Well, you're not alone. It happens to lots of us.

African violets have dark green, fuzzy leaves with slightly reddish undersides, and produce flowers that range from violet to white to pink to variegated to ruffled. There are hundreds of varieties of African violets, but all require the same care to do well.

The reason most people have trouble getting their violets to bloom is that they're not giving the plant enough light (or, sometimes, not enough food). The best location for an African violet is either a sunny windowsill with a western or southern exposure or under artificial lights for at least twelve hours a day.

Follow the care instructions below, and if your plant doesn't bloom, try gradually increasing its exposure to light.

Once you get the knack, once you set up just the right environment for your African violets, you'll be rewarded with beautiful blooms all year long.

SPECIFIC CARE REQUIREMENTS

Light: Keep your plant on either a windowsill, preferably with a western or southern exposure, or under artificial lights.

Water: Keep the soil moist, watering from below to prevent breaking and rotting stems.

Humidity: Keep the humidity high. Keep the plant on a pebble tray and mist it with tepid water to avoid leaf spotting.

Temperature: Warm. 65 to 85 degrees.

Food: Feed with (commercially available) African violet food, except during November and December, when the plant should take its seasonal rest.

Propagate from leaf cuttings or by division.

Amaryllis

HIPPEASTRUM VITTATUM

This spectacular flowering bulb plant is usually seen in great abundance around the Christmas season.

Bearing as many as five large, open, lilylike flowers on stalks that emerge from the center of darkish-green, straplike leaves, a fresh, vibrant amaryllis can take your breath away and reward you with a dazzling display of color during those gray winter months. You'll see flowers in white, red, pink, coral, and some really gorgeous variegated shades.

Most people throw their plant away after it finishes blooming, but if you save your amaryllis bulb it will bloom again.

Wait for the flowers to die and the foliage to turn yellow, which should be sometime in late spring. Then store the pot and bulb in a cool, dry place (such as a basement or garage). Make a note to check it around the end of October.

Miraculously, new foliage will have begun to appear. Bring the pot back out near a light source, start watering and fertilizing, and the blooming cycle will begin anew. To prolong the blooming as long as possible, keep the plant in bright, filtered light.

SPECIFIC CARE REQUIREMENTS

Light: Bright, indirect light.
Water: Water this plant thoroughly when it's dry.
Humidity: Medium. Spray it daily.
Temperature: Medium. 55 to 75 degrees.

To propagate, divide the bulbs every three or four years.

Anthurium
or *Flamingo Flower*

ANTHURIUM SCHERZERIANUM

This beautiful, very exotic, extremely tropical-looking plant has dark green, leathery leaves and produces heart-shaped, waxy flowers with a bright yellow spike in the center. These flowers can be red, white, or pink, and can vary in width from two inches all the way up to six or eight inches.

The keys to success with *Anthurium* include lots of light, warmth, and humidity—the closer to greenhouse conditions you can get, the more likely the *Anthurium* is to bloom. It's also critical that you use fir bark or a half soil, half peat moss potting mix. Beware of cold drafts during the winter.

It's often difficult to find exactly the right combination of elements that will get the *Anthurium* to bloom, but the plant's rich, stately foliage can be rewarding in and of itself.

SPECIFIC CARE REQUIREMENTS

Light: Bright, filtered.
Water: Keep the soil moist at all times.
Humidity: High. Mist this plant daily and keep it on a pebble tray.
Temperature: Warm. 65 to 85 degrees.
Soil: Use osmunda or fir bark.

Aphelandra
or *Zebra Plant*

APHELANDRA SQUARROSA
cv. "Louisae"

The zebra plant, with its glossy, emerald-green leaves marked with creamy white veins, can be the star of your plant menagerie. When you buy this plant it will usually be bearing a gorgeous yellow flower, spike-shaped and tipped with green.

If you give your *Aphelandra* lots of filtered western or southern sunlight and keep it moist at all times, it will bloom profusely during the fall. After the flower has died, you should cut its succulent brown stem back—to about six inches above the top of the soil. The plant won't do much over the winter, but spring will bring an abundance of new foliage. If you follow the care instructions below, the plant should produce new blooms each fall.

The one problem most people encounter with their zebra plants is lots of lower leaf droppage. The end result is a tall, stalky plant with a mere tuft of foliage at the top. In most cases this means that the plant isn't getting enough humidity. Unless you like this very sculptured look, make sure to cut the plant back (as above) after the flower has died.

SPECIFIC CARE REQUIREMENTS

Light: Bright, filtered western or southern light.
Water: Keep the soil moist.
Humidity: High. Mist this plant daily and keep it on a pebble tray.
Temperature: Warm. 65 to 85 degrees.
Soil: Peat moss or fir bark is best.

Propagate from stem cuttings.

Arrowhead Plant

SYNGONIUM PODOPHYLLUM

Also known as nephthytis, this compact, bushy plant has arrowhead-shaped light green or dark green leaves with creamy white or silver variegations. This very popular foliage plant is "most rewarding" because it will flourish practically without care. In fact, it is virtually impossible to kill. Just keep it out of western or southern light, where it will eventually turn yellow and die.

The biggest problem you'll have with your arrowhead plant is keeping it under control. You'll have to trim it fairly often so that it won't become long and straggly. Also, yellow leaves will appear frequently. They are natural and should merely be pinched off.

SPECIFIC CARE REQUIREMENTS

Light: Medium. Filtered eastern or northern exposure is fine.

Water: Water only when the soil is dry.

Humidity: Medium. Spray as often as you remember to—this will help avoid brown tips.

Temperature: Medium. 50 to 75 degrees.

Propagate from stem cuttings. These cuttings will develop roots and can be grown in water for as long as a year.

Artillery Plant

PILEA MICROPHYLLA

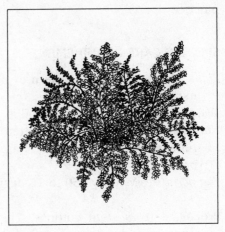

The low-growing artillery plant has very small, bright green, fleshy leaves growing profusely on soft, succulent stems. Another stunning *Pilea, P. cadierei,* is commonly called the aluminum plant. This variety is especially striking, with small, narrow, bright or bluish-green, quilted leaves, splashed with silver-aluminum streaks.

The key to success with *Pilea* is to keep the humidity around it high and not overwater—which will cause mushy stems and droopy plants. *P. microphylla* is very rewarding in a terrarium, and *P. cadierei* is a great accent in a dish garden.

SPECIFIC CARE REQUIREMENTS

Light: Filtered. Don't expose *Pilea* to direct sunlight.

Water: Keep the soil moist, but not soaking wet.

Humidity: High. For best results, keep this plant in a terrarium.

Temperature: Warm. 65 to 85 degrees.

Propagate from stem cuttings.

Asparagus Fern

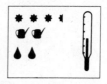

ASPARAGUS DENSIFLORUS SPRENGERII

Not really a fern, and not actually an asparagus, this durable houseplant has long, thin, bright green, fernlike stems and feathery, needlelike foliage. It makes a great hanging plant in front of a bright window or enclosed sun porch.

Another variety, *A. meyerii*, looks like erect, green "foxtails," and is most rewarding on a sunny windowsill. Both varieties will produce red and yellow berries that contain the seeds from which new plants can be grown.

Asparagus ferns are relatively easy to grow if you follow the care instructions. The key to success is to make sure that your asparagus fern gets enough light. Too little light and the needles will be falling continuously, creating an unsightly plant— not to mention a housekeeping problem.

Asparagus ferns will benefit from a summer vacation outdoors in the shade. Also, repot your asparagus fern when its bulbous roots emerge from beneath the soil. If you don't want to put it into a bigger pot, trim the root system when it gets too big.

SPECIFIC CARE REQUIREMENTS

Light: Bright. A slightly filtered southern exposure is perfect.

Water: Water only when the soil begins to dry out.

Humidity: Medium. A daily misting helps keep the plant fresh and healthy.

Temperature: Medium. 50 to 70 degrees.

Propagate by division or from seeds.

Australian Umbrella Tree or *Schefflera*

BRASSAIA ACTINOPHYLLA

Whether you call it an umbrella tree or a schefflera, or even if you mispronounce it "sheffleria" (which most people do), this plant is a great choice for a bright, airy location where an outdoorsy, treelike plant is called for. Its woody branches hold rosettes of dark green, leathery leaves that form the shape of an open umbrella. In its native habitat the schefflera can grow up to one hundred feet tall.

The most common problem indoor gardeners encounter with this plant is leaf drop, which is usually due either to cold drafts, not enough light, or overwatering. If you come home to find leaves all over the floor, try adjusting your care—see if you can put the plant where it will get a little more light, try cutting back on your watering, and make sure to keep the front door closed.

SPECIFIC CARE REQUIREMENTS

Light: Bright. The more light the merrier. A southern or western exposure is best.
Water: Let the soil dry out between waterings.
Humidity: Medium. Spray this plant daily.
Temperature: Warm. Between 65 and 85 degrees.

Propagate from stem cuttings.

Azalea

RHODODENDRON *spp.*

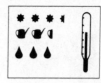

There are dozens of species and varieties (some hybrids) of azalea. They differ only in the size and the color of the small, multipetaled, roselike flowers that blossom forth in a multitude of colors—including red, pink, and white. The narrow, slightly oval leaves are dark green and somewhat fuzzy, and the stems are very woody. Some varieties of azalea will grow up to five or six feet tall, while others will only be one to two feet tall.

For years I was skeptical about growing azaleas indoors, even though they're gorgeous flowering accents and a great gift plant. I used to recommend that if you received or purchased a potted azalea you should, if at all possible, plant it outdoors, where it will flourish in almost any climate for years and years.

Now, from repeated personal success, I can tell you that although your azalea will be dormant during late fall and winter, it will produce dazzling blooms year after year indoors. Make sure that it gets good, bright western or southern light, and feed it with an acid fertilizer during the spring and summer. It's also a good idea to prune your azalea at the end of its blooming season. This will encourage lush new growth and ensure flowering the following season.

SPECIFIC CARE REQUIREMENTS

Light: Bright. Remember, all flowering plants need lots of light.

Water: Keep the soil slightly moist. Cut back on watering during the dormant season.

Humidity: High. Mist this plant often and keep it on a pebble tray.

Temperature: Medium. 50 to 70 degrees.

Propagate from stem cuttings.

Baby's Tears

HELXINE SOLEIROLI

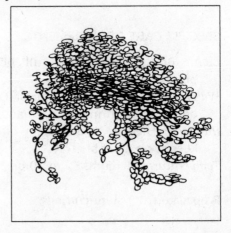

This creeping herb forms dense, bushy clumps of tiny, round, slightly succulent green leaves.

Since the key to success with this plant is high humidity, baby's tears is a perfect candidate for a terrarium, where it will thrive. I remember growing baby's tears in a five-gallon water bottle terrarium and having a very small plant grow all the way out of the bottle inside of a year!

Baby's tears will also function nicely as a hanging plant in a bright, airy location, developing long, trailing shoots. If you're growing this plant in a hanging basket, water it by lifting the shoots and watering directly into the soil—so as not to rot the crown of the plant—or water from the bottom of the pot.

Again, the key is humidity. If you don't give your baby's tears enough, it will quickly become a sorrowful plant—dry, yellow, straggly, and sparse.

There is another plant that's always sold as baby's tears—it's very much like *H. soleiroli*, except that it's a brighter green color and its leaves are larger—about a quarter of an inch in diameter—and more succulent. It looks, to me at least, like it should be growing in a lawn. Anyway, this plant, which requires the same care as *H. soleiroli*, is known botanically as *Pilea depressa*.

Just thought you might like to know.

SPECIFIC CARE REQUIREMENTS

Light: Bright light if hanging, but indirect light if in a terrarium.

Water: Keep the soil slightly moist at all times.

Humidity: High. If hanging, baby's tears must be misted daily

Temperature: Warm. 65 to 85 degrees.

Propagate from stem cuttings.

Banana Tree

MUSA *spp.*

"Yes, we have no bananas," goes the old tune. But you can change that perky old tune to "Yes, I have lots of bananas," if you purchase a banana plant and cultivate it properly.

You've certainly seen pictures of these tall, slender beauties: long, wide, light green leaves emerging from the top of the thick stems. The edges of the leaves are usually torn slightly as protection against stiff tropical breezes.

Keep this plant in bright, filtered light (a direct southern exposure would burn it up), keep the soil moist, and most important, spray it every day—the banana tree needs *lots* of humidity.

A banana tree is most rewarding as a decorative addition to a lanai room or an atrium. Here's a bonus: If you do manage to provide perfect circumstances, your banana tree will eventually bear fruit.

SPECIFIC CARE REQUIREMENTS

Light: Bright, but slightly filtered western or southern sunlight.

Water: Keep the soil moist.

Humidity: Medium high. Spray this plant at least once daily.

Temperature: Warm. 65 to 85 degrees. Do beware of cold drafts during winter.

Propagate from rhizomes (thick, rooted underground stems—which you'll have to buy) or from offsets (small plantlets) that appear at the base of the plant.

Begonia

There are hundreds of different types of begonias. Some are grown from tubers or rhizomes, others from fibrous roots.

Real begonia fanciers belong to clubs and societies and grow many different varieties. Some varieties, such as the Angel-Wing or the spectacular Iron Cross—with its fuzzy, green leaves marked by a distinct dark brown German cross—are grown primarily for their striking foliage, while others are grown for their tiny blooms. I've seen begonias at plant shows that are absolutely breathtaking—huge globes of perfect foliage covered with dazzling clusters of pink, red, or white blossoms.

The "basic" begonia is probably *B. semperflorens*, or wax begonia. It has light green or brownish waxy foliage and bears small, pretty pink flowers. This plant is usually sold in the spring or summer as an outdoor annual. It can be cultivated indoors by following the instructions below and feeding it every two or three weeks with a commercial plant food.

Begonia Rex

But the begonia I like best is the *elatior* variety, or Rieger begonia, which is grown for its profusion of roselike blooms. This particular variety has light green, shiny, oval leaves and produces small but beautiful rosette-shaped flowers in coral, yellow, and red.

It will bloom all year if properly tended: The keys are giving it bright, filtered light and keeping the soil slightly moist. But beware of mildew—which is a common problem when this begonia doesn't get enough air circulation. Mildew will appear as a white, powdery substance on the leaves, and can be cured by applying any commercial fungicide.

Begonia Elatior

SPECIFIC CARE REQUIREMENTS

Light: Bright, filtered light.
Water: Allow the soil to dry out between waterings.
Humidity: High. Spray the plant daily and keep it on a pebble tray.
Temperature: Medium. 55 to 75 degrees.

Propagate from leaf cuttings.

Bird-of-paradise
STRELITZIA REGINAE

I'm sure you've seen this plant—with its long, leathery, blue-gray leaves; thick, tall stems; and spectacular flowers: boat-shaped green bracts topped by spiky orange-and-blue flowers and a purple tongue. This is truly a regal, flowering bird.

If you live in Hawaii, California, or Florida you've probably got this plant growing in your backyard. If you live anywhere else you can grow the bird-of-paradise in your living room, as long as you can provide lots of good, bright sun. It takes at least six or seven years for a bird-of-paradise to bloom indoors, so patience is not only a virtue, it's a must. Once it starts blooming, though, it'll bloom year after year.

SPECIFIC CARE REQUIREMENTS

Light: Bright light. The more western or southern sunlight the merrier.
Water: Keep the soil moist.
Humidity: High. Spray it daily and keep it on a pebble tray.
Temperature: Medium. 55 to 75 degrees.

Propagate by division.

Bird's-nest Fern

ASPLENIUM NIDUS

I love this plant. Its beautiful rosette of spreading bright green fronds, and the ever-present new fronds unfurling from its brown, almost mossy center, make it a very interesting and very beautiful plant.

Although most bird's-nest ferns are just medium-sized when sold—in six- or eight-inch pots—I've also seen really huge ones that are at least five or six feet tall and wide enough to make an ostrich comfortable.

This plant needs filtered eastern or northern light, but high humidity is critical. You don't need greenhouse conditions, but without enough humidity the edges of the leaves will turn brown and unsightly quickly. Keep the plant near a humidifier if possible. Remember: Like all ferns, this plant likes lots of water.

You propagate this plant by sowing the spores that will appear on the undersides of the fronds. These will look like neat rows of round black objects. Lightly scrape them off into a paper bag, and let them dry in the bag for three days. Then plant them in a tray of damp vermiculite. Keep the tray warm and the spores should germinate within two or three weeks.

SPECIFIC CARE REQUIREMENTS

Light: Indirect light. A northern exposure is perfect, and filtered eastern light is acceptable.

Water: Keep the soil moist at all times.

Humidity: High. Spray this plant twice a day, morning and evening, and keep it near a humidifier if possible.

Temperature: Medium. 55 to 75 degrees.

Propagate by sowing the spores that appear on the undersides of the fronds.

Bloodleaf Plant

IRISINE HERBSTII

This is a very showy plant, practically the only bright red foliage plant I can think of. (There's coleus and croton—but their foliage is usually variegated with lots of other colors.) The bloodleaf has small, heart-shaped, dark red leaves—with pink veins and a pink midrib—which grow on succulent stems.

Some books will tell you that this is an easy plant to grow. Over the years I've had several, and despite frequent pinching back, they've usually gotten straggly—long and leggy with sparse, small foliage—and just weren't worth saving.

But I've kept several going for months and months, and since they're colorful and inexpensive, I think the bloodleaf plant can be very rewarding.

The keys to success are proper light and watering. A shop in my neighborhood has one flourishing in a southeast exposure. At the end of a hot, two-day period during which the shop was closed, I noticed the plant had drooped completely for lack of water. Within hours of the shop's re-opening and the plant's being watered, it was back standing tall and straight, good as new.

SPECIFIC CARE REQUIREMENTS

Light: Bright light. If you don't give the plant enough sun, its color will fade.

Water: Allow the soil to dry out between waterings.

Humidity: Medium. Spray this plant daily.

Temperature: Medium. 55 to 75 degrees.

Propagate from stem cuttings.

Boston Fern

NEPHROLEPSIS EXALTATA BOSTONIENSIS

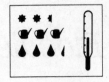

I am known far and wide as the Boston Fern Strangler. I've had absolutely no luck with this plant. But follow my care instructions and *you* will, because just about everybody I've ever instructed has burgeoning Boston ferns.

Although the Boston fern can tolerate higher temperatures than most ferns, dry heat can be deadly. Give your Boston fern a bright, cool location—a northern window or a filtered eastern exposure is perfect.

Water it thoroughly at least once a week. Let it just barely dry out, and then water it thoroughly again. When watering, lift the fronds and water directly into the soil so as not to rot the fronds at the crown. Mist daily—ferns need lots of humidity.

Cut away any dead fronds at each watering. These are natural—old fronds die off to make room for new growth. The threadlike runners that the Boston fern sends out are supposed to produce buds, then new plants. But it rarely happens indoors, so cut them off if you like.

The key to succeeding with a Boston fern is to hang it or put it on a stand. Never set it on the floor, a table, or a shelf. The plant needs adequate air circulation: The fronds must be able to breathe or the plant will quickly dry up and turn brown.

Here's another tip: If you've got an outdoor area and live in a moderate climate, buy *two* Boston ferns and rotate them. Keep one outdoors in the shade for a week while the other graces your breakfast area or bathroom. Then reverse them. A biweekly outdoor spring and summer vacation really perks up a fern.

SPECIFIC CARE REQUIREMENTS

Light: Bright and cool light. A northern window or a filtered eastern exposure is perfect.

Water: Water this plant thoroughly, as instructed above.

Humidity: High. Spray it every day.

Temperature: Medium. 50 to 70 degrees.

Propagate by division.

Buddhist Pine

PODOCARPUS MACROPHYLLUS

Also known as the southern yew, this is a much underrated houseplant. I wish Buddhist pines were more easily available, because it's one of the few conifers that will do well indoors.

A conifer is an evergreen, pinelike shrub or tree with spiny, thin needles—as opposed to leaves. All conifers, however, are not necessarily pines. To get to the point, the Buddhist pine is a conifer, but not a true pine, which makes it a good houseplant—since true pines need a cold, hard dormancy outdoors during the winter.

Anyway, with its delicate needles on large branches, this plant looks very similar to a small Christmas tree. Most of the Buddhist pines I've stumbled across (and bought) over the years have been small—about six inches tall. They'll grow to be about two feet high if you keep them in bright light, keep the soil moist, spray them daily, and keep the temperature between 55 and 75 degrees.

If you can find a *P. macrophyllus*, I think you'll enjoy having it as part of your plant collection. And to that person who once asked me why this plant is called the "Buddhist" pine—I don't have the faintest idea.

SPECIFIC CARE REQUIREMENTS

Light: Bright. A western or southern windowsill would be best.
Water: Keep the soil moist.
Humidity: Medium. Spray this plant daily.
Temperature: Medium. 55 to 75 degrees.

Propagate from stem cuttings.

Burro's Tail
or Donkey's Tail

SEDUM MORGANIANUM

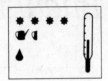

The burro's tail can be very rewarding hanging in a sun room or a bright kitchen window. A native of Mexico, this plant is a lovely hanging succulent with tassels of short, spindle-shaped, light green leaves. (I've never seen a burro with a light green tail, but there is a definite resemblance.)

When I think of burros, I think of plodding, straight-ahead, dependable creatures, and the burro's tail plant fits that description. Give it lots of sun—a western or southern exposure—and it will slowly get bigger and bigger and the "tails" will get longer and longer. Not enough sun, and the individual leaves will start dropping off.

This plant is a must for the serious cactus-and-succulent collector.

SPECIFIC CARE REQUIREMENTS

Light: Bright western or southern sunlight.
Water: Allow the soil to dry out thoroughly between waterings.
Humidity: Low. Spray it once a week.
Temperature: Medium. 50 to 70 degrees.

Propagate from stem cuttings.

Busy Lizzie
or *Patient Lucy*

IMPATIENS SULTANI

Frankly, I only grow *Impatiens* as an outdoor annual. I plant them in the spring and let them run their natural course through the summer. But many of my friends grow them indoors all year around. They are greatly rewarded by the beautiful, clover-shaped, red, pink, white, or coral-colored flowers—surrounded by oblong green (or yellow-and-green) leaves on succulent stems. Give an *Impatiens* a spot in bright, filtered sunlight, keep it damp, and see if you have as much luck as my friends.

After they finish blooming outdoors, *Impatiens* can be brought indoors, potted in commercial potting mix, cut back when they begin dropping their leaves, and cultivated (as below) in a sunny window. Or they can be stored by hanging them upside-down in a cool, dry place, then bringing them out and repotting them in the spring.

The key to growing *Impatiens* is having patience. Watching them just sit there from December through April can make for a long winter.

SPECIFIC CARE REQUIREMENTS

Light: Bright, filtered light.
Water: Keep the soil damp.
Humidity: Medium. Spray this plant daily.
Temperature: Medium. 55 to 75 degrees.
Soil: Use fir bark or peat moss for best results.

Propagate from stem cuttings or seeds.

Button Fern

PELLAEA ROTUNDIFOLIA

I thought this plant was right up there in difficulty with the maidenhair fern until I saw a friend of mine grow one on a shelf in a northern window. It's still doing fine, and it's been three years since he brought it home.

The button fern is really a very attractive plant—low-growing and spreading, with small, round, dark green leaves and fuzzy stems. As with most ferns, the key to success is giving the plant lots of humidity. Otherwise it will wither up and die within a few weeks after purchase.

I now confidently recommend this fern for low-light situations, as long as you're willing to watch it carefully and give it the TLC it needs.

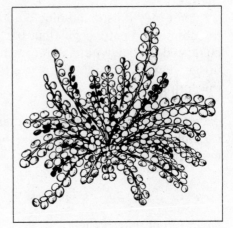

SPECIFIC CARE REQUIREMENTS

Light: Indirect light. A northern exposure is best.
Water: Keep the soil slightly damp at all times.
Humidity: High. Spray this plant daily and keep it on a pebble tray.
Temperature: Medium. 55 to 75 degrees.

Propagate by division.

Caladium

CALADIUM *cultivars*

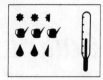

The caladium is a glamorous, spectacular, very showy plant with large, heart-shaped, crepelike leaves splashed with an infinite variety of greens, pinks, reds, whites, and creams.

Caladiums are grown from tubers (underground stems with eyes or buds), which means that they'll go dormant after they finish their spring and summer display. They'll come back to full grandeur after overwintering—without water—in a cool, dry spot. So don't despair when the new foliage gets smaller and smaller and eventually stops. It shall return!

The keys to keeping this gorgeous coffee table plant thriving as long as possible are *indirect* light and lots of water and humidity. Feed this plant with commercial houseplant food every week during the spring and summer for optimum leaf production.

Caladiums are so beautiful you'll be tempted to buy two or three new ones every season. And why not? Like fingerprints, no two are ever alike.

SPECIFIC CARE REQUIREMENTS

Light: Bright but filtered light. Keep the burning sun away from this delicate plant.

Water: Keep the soil moist.

Humidity: Medium. Spray this plant daily.

Temperature: Medium. 55 to 70 degrees.

Propagate from tubers or by division.

Calla Lily

ZANTEDESCHIA AETHIOPICA COMPACTA

"Ah, the calla lillies are in bloom...." Katharine Hepburn said that in a movie, but you'll be able to say it, too, if you buy a calla lily and take proper care of it.

Grown from a rhizome (which, like a tuber, is an underground stem with buds), the calla lily blooms in the late fall and winter, and then goes dormant from spring through summer.

This plant is a bit temperamental and needs almost greenhouse conditions to bloom. The key word is "almost." You *can* succeed with a calla lily if you experiment with levels of heat and humidity until you reach an almost marshy-type atmosphere. After dormancy, move your plant to a bright, filtered location such as an east window. Keep it on a pebble tray, keep the soil moist, spray it as often as you can when foliage appears, and make sure the temperature stays above 65 degrees.

The result will be a bushy plant about two feet tall with fleshy-stalked, glossy green leaves, which will produce spectacular funnel-shaped spaths, or "flowers," in white, pink, or yellow. If you buy your calla lily already in bloom, follow the care instructions below to ensure that it blooms as long as possible before dormancy.

SPECIFIC CARE REQUIREMENTS

Light: Bright, filtered light. An eastern window is perfect.

Water: Keep the soil moist while the plant is blooming, dry during dormancy.

Humidity: High. Keep this plant on a pebble tray and spray it frequently—at least once or twice a day.

Temperature: Warm. 65 to 85 degrees.

Propagate from offsets.

Camellia

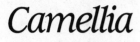

CAMELLIA JAPONICA

The camellia is an evergreen tree with woody branches and dark green, shiny, leathery, serrated leaves. In the South it's commonly grown outdoors, but it can be grown indoors anywhere.

The camellia is prized for its gorgeous, six-inch-wide, multipetaled, gardenia-like blooms, which can be white, pink, or red. These flowers usually emerge in late fall or winter. Alas, they just look like gardenia flowers—they don't smell like them. In fact, they have no fragrance at all.

The real key to camellia care might be coolness—of temperature, that is. Camellias do not tolerate heat well, and like the southern belles they are, they're likely to get "the vapors" if the temperature rises to over 75 degrees.

Camellia trees are a beautiful, decorative addition to a bright corner—they need lots of bright, filtered light to do well. I have a friend with twin pink-flowering camellias—one on either side of the entrance to her dining room. They look simply sensational all year.

SPECIFIC CARE REQUIREMENTS

Light: Bright, filtered light.
Water: Keep the soil moist.
Humidity: High. Spray this plant daily and keep it on a pebble tray or near a humidifier.
Temperature: Cool. 55 to 75 degrees.

Propagate from stem cuttings.

Cape Primrose

STREPTOCARPUS

spp. and hybrids

A very dependable flowering plant, the Cape primrose is small and stemless, with long, narrow, fuzzy leaves. Grown in bright, filtered light and kept moist, it will produce trumpetlike flowers of lavender and purple on and off all year long.

The key to success with primroses is providing enough light. If you haven't got enough light during the winter, you can keep the Cape primrose blooming by giving it twelve hours of artificial light per day. Without enough light, the plant will simply shrivel up and die.

I speak from firsthand experience: When my editors at *Redbook* asked me to include Cape primrose in an article about flowering plants, I decided to give it a try in "Mr. Mother Earth's Test Kitchen." Not only has my Cape primrose survived, but, three years later, it's still producing blooms.

SPECIFIC CARE REQUIREMENTS

Light: Bright, filtered light.
Water: Keep the soil moist.
Humidity: High. Spray this plant frequently
   and keep it on a pebble tray.
Temperature: Medium. 55 to 70 degrees.

Propagate from leaf cuttings in spring.

Cast-iron Plant

ASPIDISTRA ELATIOR

The cast-iron plant has earned its nickname through hundreds of years of durable, dependable indoor growing—with minimal light, water, and care. The plant can take very shady conditions, but some filtered eastern light would be ideal.

Although they grow slowly, *Aspidistras* will get up to three or four feet tall. Their erect, slender stems bear long, dark green oblong leaves.

Once the most popular of houseplants, *Aspidistras* are difficult to find these days, so if you see one, grab it. There's also a variegated variety painted with creamy stripes that's really pretty. If you see these, grab two!

The reward you'll get from growing *Aspidistra*? At last—a lovely, living plant for that dark corner that really, really needed it!

SPECIFIC CARE REQUIREMENTS

Light: Moderate light.

Water: Let the soil dry out between waterings.

Humidity: Medium. Spray as often as you think about it.

Temperature: Medium. Between 50 and 75 degrees.

Propagate by division.

Chenille Plant

ACALYPHA HISPIDA

This truly spectacular shrub has large, oval, bright green, hairy leaves. It produces groups of bright red flowers that have a texture like chenille and hang down in long, pendant spikes. Another variety has maroon leaves with a red border. A lush, profusely blooming chenille plant is bound to draw "oohs" and "aahs" of admiration.

The keys to success with chenille plants, as with all flowering plants, are good, bright sunlight, lots of humidity, and regular watering and feeding. In short, lots of attention and TLC. For best results, and to ensure flowering, cut this plant back in the early spring.

SPECIFIC CARE REQUIREMENTS

Light: Bright, or at the very least bright, filtered sunlight.

Water: Keep the soil moist.

Humidity: High. Spray it daily and keep it on a pebble tray.

Temperature: Medium to warm. 60 to 80 degrees.

Propagate from stem cuttings.

Chinese Evergreen

AGLAONEMA MODESTUM

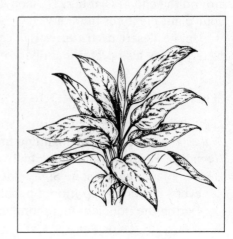

This is another easy-to-care-for but most rewarding plant. You'll see Chinese evergreens in virtually every nursery and garden center—in fact, almost everywhere plants are sold—and well you should. When it comes to combining durability with decorative usefulness, this plant is hard to beat.

The true *Aglaonema* is plain green, but *A. modestum variegatum*, with its leathery, grayish-green, lance-shaped leaves splattered with creamy or silver variegation, is the most common variety.

Care for all varieties—and there are dozens—is the same: easy. One of the distinct decorating pluses is that all Chinese evergreens will do well in low light. In fact, if you give them too much light the leaves will turn pale yellow. Water them only when the soil dries out.

All of the varieties will produce white spathes—leaflike structures that enclose a white flower cluster—and colorful red, yellow, and orange berries.

SPECIFIC CARE REQUIREMENTS

Light: Does very well in low light.
Water: Allow the soil to dry out between waterings.
Humidity: Medium. Spray this plant daily.
Temperature: Medium. 50 to 75 degrees.

Propagate from stem cuttings.

Christmas Cactus

SCHLUMBERGERA BRIDGESII

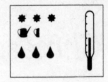

Similar to the Thanksgiving cactus *(S. truncata)*, and often confused with the Easter cactus *(Rhipsalidopsis gaertneri)*, this branching epiphytic plant has small, green, leaflike stems. (An epiphytic plant takes its nourishment from the air, not the soil.) Depending on the variety, the Christmas cactus will produce bell-like flowers from the tips of the stems in December or in the early fall. The flowers are usually red or white and only last a few days.

The most common complaints I hear about these terrestrial cacti are: (1) my Christmas cactus doesn't bloom, and (2) the buds form, but they fall off before they open.

In order to get any cactus to bloom, you must give it lots of bright light during the day and try to see that it gets at least twelve hours of darkness at night starting around the end of October. To keep Christmas cactus buds from dropping off, give your plant plenty of humidity.

Unlike desert cacti, terrestrial cacti should not be allowed to dry out completely. They also prefer loam-based potting soil to sandy soil.

SPECIFIC CARE REQUIREMENTS

Light: Bright, filtered light.
Water: Keep the soil just slightly damp.
Humidity: Keep the humidity high during the blooming season. Spray the plant every day and keep it on a pebble tray. During the nonblooming months, spray it every three or four days.
Temperature: Medium during the day, but during winter nights the temperature should be kept cooler to encourage blooming. This plant likes temperatures around 40 to 45 degrees at night during the winter.

Propagate from stem cuttings.

Coffee Plant

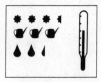

COFFEA ARABICA

About three years ago I bought some *unroasted* coffee beans and planted a few about an inch down in regular potting mix. All but two germinated within three weeks, and today I've got a veritable coffee plantation on the windowsill of my kitchen.

This row of plants, with woody stems and dark green, shiny leaves, stands as testimony that you neither have to be Juan Valdez nor live in a tropical climate to grow coffee.

I think growing a plant from your grocery bag can be tremendously rewarding. If you follow the care instructions carefully, giving the plant bright light and watering it frequently, your coffee plant should produce white flowers—which will be followed by bright red berries—after three or four years. If you want your coffee plant to get full and bushy, prune it back two or three inches in late March.

Inside the berries are the seeds, or "beans," that are roasted to make coffee. My plants haven't bloomed yet, but I'll bet someday they'll yield at least a demitasse.

SPECIFIC CARE REQUIREMENTS

Light: Bright. Give the plants a western or southern exposure.
Water: Moist. Don't let the plant dry out.
Humidity: Moderate. Mist the plant daily.
Temperature: Medium to warm. The temperature shouldn't drop below 55 degrees.

Propagate from stem cuttings, seeds, or unroasted coffee beans.

Coleus

COLEUS *spp.*

For sheer spectacular colorful beauty, it's hard to match the foliage of the coleus.

Coleus has very thin, delicate leaves, usually serrated, that grow on fleshy stems and range in color from deep maroon to bright red, green, or are variegated with red, green, and yellow.

You'll see two kinds: a larger-leafed, erect variety, which is used as an annual for outdoor plantings or as a flashy bit of windowsill decor; and a trailing, smaller-leafed variety commonly seen in hanging baskets.

Keep it in bright, filtered light, water it often, and pinch it back regularly, and your coleus will produce stalks of pretty blue flowers during the spring and summer months.

The key to keeping your coleus bushy and healthy is to constantly pinch back new growth. This prevents the plant from becoming straggly—otherwise you'll end up with long, leggy vines and sparse foliage—
very unsightly!

SPECIFIC CARE REQUIREMENTS

Light: Bright, filtered light. A summer vacation outside in the shade is particularly good for coleus.
Water: Keep the soil moist.
Humidity: Medium. Spray this plant daily.
Temperature: Medium. 55 to 75 degrees. Too much heat and this plant will wither right up.

Propagate from stem cuttings.

Corn Plant

DRACAENA FRAGRANS MASSANGEANA

Tried-and-true indoor plants, corn plants are often seen in hotel lobbies or banks, where they thrive under nothing but artificial light. You'll also find them in shady corners in homes and apartments, where they are one of the most rewarding of all decorative indoor trees.

Given indirect light and watered only when dry, corn plants will grow into thick, round stalks called canes. These are topped off with tufts of long, wide, pointed green leaves that have a chartreuse or light green stripe down the middle.

If you don't give your corn plant enough humidity, the plant's leaves will develop brown tips and the lower leaves will drop. It's difficult to combat this condition, but spraying your corn plant daily can help delay the inevitable. The brown tips can be manicured off with a pair of scissors, but as long as there's healthy new growth emerging from the top of your corn plant it's doing fine.

When your corn plant gets too tall it can be air-layered (see "Propagating"), and you'll have two plants from the one you started with.

SPECIFIC CARE REQUIREMENTS

Light: Indirect light. Too much light will fade this plant.
Water: Allow the soil to dry out between waterings.
Humidity: Medium. Spray this plant daily.
Temperature: Medium. 50 to 75 degrees.

Propagate by air-layering or stem cuttings.

Creeping Fig
or Climbing Fig

FICUS PUMILA

This quite pretty member of the fig family is very rewarding as a hanging plant and absolutely the perfect plant for covering topiary frames (see "Topiary").

Its small, dark green leaves are quilted on top and rough on the undersides. Each leaf is small and delicate, only about a quarter of an inch across. The leaves are densely bunched, which gives the plant a soft, cushiony look.

Creeping fig is easy to care for: The key is to give it no more than filtered eastern light—too much bright sun will dry this plant up. In fact, this plant is so durable that you can even use it in a northern exposure. Just be careful when you water—which should be often enough to keep the soil moist. Like most plants with thick crowns, you should lift the foliage and water directly into the soil (or water from the bottom) to prevent a bald spot from developing in the crown.

If you've got a topiary figure covered with creeping fig, you should dunk it completely once a week.

SPECIFIC CARE REQUIREMENTS

Light: Filtered eastern light, or even only northern light is fine.
Water: Keep the soil moist. Lift trailing foliage and water directly into the soil to prevent crown rot.
Humidity: Medium. Spray this plant daily.
Temperature: Medium. 55 to 75 degrees.

Propagate from stem cuttings.

Croton

CODIAEUM VARIEGATUM AND CULTIVARS

In *Mother Earth's Hassle-Free Indoor Plant Book*, I talked about crotons being "glamour plants"—gorgeous, irresistible plants that weren't really suitable for indoor growing.

With the passage of time and with lots more experience I've learned that crotons, although still as glamorous as ever, are easy to cultivate indoors. In fact, I've got two beauties on my living room windowsill that have been flourishing now for at least three years.

Crotons are grown for their extraordinary foliage. They are tropical shrubs with blazingly beautiful ornamental leaves. Thick, leathery, and sometimes twisted into spirals, these leaves are variegated in never-ending rainbows of exquisite colors—predominantly greens, reds, and yellows.

The key to growing crotons successfully is to give them lots of light and humidity. The proper combination of these two elements will prevent the lower leaves from dropping off—which is the biggest problem you'll encounter with this plant. Follow the directions below and experiment with different levels of light, watering, and humidity until you reach the proper balance of elements for your room and your plant.

Oh, and watch your crotons carefully during the summer—they tend to wilt in the heat. A thorough watering will help correct this condition.

SPECIFIC CARE REQUIREMENTS

Light: Bright, filtered light.

Water: Keep the soil slightly damp, especially during the hot summer months, when this plant is especially thirsty.

Humidity: Medium-high. Spray this plant at least once daily. Keep it on a pebble tray for best results.

Temperature: Medium to warm. 60 to 85 degrees.

Propagate from stem cuttings.

Crown-of-thorns

EUPHORBIA SPLENDENS

This ancient succulent, which I'm sure you're familiar with because of its biblical connotations, isn't really all that attractive—fortunately, its flowers are beautiful.

It's a very easy plant to grow, as long as you give it lots of sunlight and don't overwater. A friend of mine even has one flourishing on an office windowsill.

The crown-of-thorns will grow up to three feet high, its stems covered with sharp, throny spikes and small, oval leaves. The plant also produces pretty red cloverlike flowers on and off all year long. Even during the winter months, when it's bare of leaves, the crown-of-thorns may be covered with flowers. And what could be more rewarding than that?

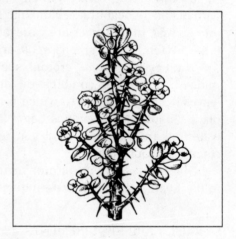

SPECIFIC CARE REQUIREMENTS

Light: Bright light. Like all cacti and succulents, this plant needs lots of sunlight.
Water: Allow the soil to dry out between waterings, even when in bloom.
Humidity: Medium. Spray this plant daily.
Temperature: Medium. 50 to 75 degrees.

Propagate from stem cuttings.

Cyclamen

CYCLAMEN PERSICUM

You will begin to see cyclamens in nurseries and flower shops around the beginning of November, and you'll continue to see them through the end of January.

This low-growing winter bloomer has round, gray-green leaves with a very attractive silver design. It produces lovely, delicate, butterfly-shaped red, white, or pink flowers on the ends of fleshy stalks that are four to five inches long.

To prolong blooming, and to keep the foliage looking its best during the growing season, keep the plant in bright, filtered light, keep the soil damp—and, most important, keep the plant *cool*. Cyclamens relish temperatures as low as 40 degrees at night.

Most people despair when their cyclamen "dies" around the middle of February. Take heart—it's only resting. Cyclamen grows from tubers, and can be stored during its dormant period.

When your cyclamen's foliage turns yellow, take the pot to a cool, dry place and leave it there until October. Bring it out again, begin watering, and gradually move it closer and closer to a good bright light source. By December it should be in full bloom again. Or, to save storage space, you can unpot the tuber, store it in a plastic bag in a drawer, and then repot it in fresh soil in October.

SPECIFIC CARE REQUIREMENTS

Light: Bright, filtered light.
Water: Keep the soil damp.
Humidity: High. Spray it at least once a day
    and keep it on a pebble tray.
Temperature: Cool. 40 to 60 degrees.

Propagate by division.

Date Palm

PHOENIX ROEBELENI

The date palm is a very graceful houseplant with a single, rough trunk topped by a crown of feathery leaves. It can grow up to sixty to seventy feet tall in its natural habitat, but this dwarf variety will only reach about three or four feet indoors.

Although an established plant is expensive to buy, you can grow one yourself from the pit of an *unpasteurized* date. (You can usually find these in health food stores.) Plant several pits about an inch deep in a four-inch pot filled with one-half commercial potting mix and one-half vermiculite. Keep the mixture moist and the pot warm (between 65 and 80 degrees). Then, because it takes quite a while for a date palm seed to germinate, months perhaps, be patient.

Keep the plant in filtered eastern light, keep the soil moist, spray it frequently, and in about five years you'll have a nice, mature tree. For best results keep this plant potbound. Like all palms, the date palm likes its roots to be tightly contained, so avoid the temptation to use anything larger than a ten-inch pot for repotting.

Fighting valiantly to forgo any puns, let me just say that you'll never get any dates from your homegrown date palm.

SPECIFIC CARE REQUIREMENTS

Light: Filtered eastern light is perfect.
Water: Keep the soil moist.
Humidity: Medium. Spray this plant daily.
Temperature: Warm. Between 60 and 85 degrees is best. Beware of cold drafts.

Propagate from offsets or from the pits of unpasteurized dates.

Devil's Ivy or Pothos

SCINDAPSUS AUREUS

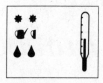

I have seven of these plants either hanging or sitting in shady locations, and I love them all for their constant, healthy growth.

Commonly called pothos, this first cousin to the philodendron is a true champion among easy-to-care-for plants. With its broad, oval, waxy leaves, green with yellow or white markings, the pothos can withstand low light, dry conditions, and semineglect.

It should be cut back from time to time to encourage full, bushy growth—the cuttings can be grown in water for as long as a year. This plant will do remarkably well in low light, but the white or yellow variegations will fail to appear on new growth if the plant is in a very shady spot. Your pothos will droop noticeably when it needs water.

Interestingly, of my seven pothos plants, the one sitting atop the stereo—which has been playing lots of classical music lately—is doing the best of all.

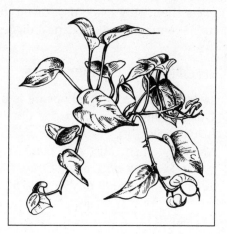

SPECIFIC CARE REQUIREMENTS

Light: Filtered light.
Water: Medium.
Humidity: Medium. Spray it daily to help prevent the leaf tips from turning brown.
Temperature: Medium. 50 to 75 degrees.

Propagate from stem cuttings.

Dumbcane

DIEFFENBACHIA *spp.*

This plant's name reflects the fact that the leaves and stem of the dieffenbachia contain toxins that, if ingested, can temporarily damage the larynx and leave you literally speechless. Keep this plant *away* from small children or pets who tend to nibble on plants.

But the dumbcane is a very rewarding plant to grow, because all of the varieties look very glamorous—with unique and splashy patterns and designs. And all are enormously useful for basic home decor.

You'll see many different species of dumbcane: *D. amoena* has thick stems with large, oblong, pointed leaves marked with creamy white splotches. The other commercially available varieties, including *D. roehrsii*, *D. picta*, and *D. oerstedii*, have leaves with slightly different shapes and slightly different markings.

The care for all dumbcanes is the same: Give them filtered eastern light and water them only when dry. Given these basic conditions, high humidity is the key to preventing the dumbcane's biggest problem—loss of its lower leaves.

SPECIFIC CARE REQUIREMENTS

Light: Filtered eastern exposure is perfect.

Water: Allow the soil to dry out between waterings.

Humidity: High. Mist this plant frequently and keep it on a pebble tray.

Temperature: Medium. 55 to 75 degrees. Cold drafts will cause brown and rotting leaves.

Propagate with stem cuttings or by air-layering.

Dwarf Lemon

CITRUS LIMON *"meyerii"*

This plant is a hybrid of lemon and orange—and, like all citrus plants, is very easy to grow as a houseplant. You can either buy an established citrus plant or grow one from the seeds of your own oranges, lemons, or grapefruits. To my mind, growing your own is infinitely more rewarding. (See "Plants from Pits.")

Citrus trees have woody stems and bright shiny leaves, and will produce very fragrant white flowers. They'll eventually bear edible fruit—edible at least in the case of *C. limon* "meyerii."

The key to succeeding with citrus plants is to give them bright light and to feed them once a week during the spring and summer. Taking your citrus outside—to a half sunny, half shady location—during the late spring or summer will help stimulate flower and fruit growth.

SPECIFIC CARE REQUIREMENTS

Light: Bright. A western or southern exposure is best.
Water: Keep the soil moist.
Humidity: Medium. Spray this plant daily.
Temperature: Medium. 55 to 70 degrees. Watch out for cold drafts during the winter.

Propagate from seeds or stem cuttings.

Dwarf Myrtle

MYRTUS COMMUNIS

This is a great plant to shape into a small standard, because it has a woody stem and grows no taller than three feet high. It's a bushy shrub with small, shiny, dark green leaves that produces very fragrant white flowers during the spring, summer, and most of the fall.

I have a dwarf myrtle on my living room windowsill—and new buds appear nearly every day. I water it practically every day during the summer because it dries out in its bright western exposure, and I feed it once a week starting in May, right through September. I'm rewarded with tons of blooms. In fact, I can practically see new buds forming as I write this.

SPECIFIC CARE REQUIREMENTS

Light: Bright. A western or southern exposure is necessary to ensure blooming.

Water: Allow the soil to dry out, then water thoroughly. During the hot summer months you may have to water a little every day, but you'll be able to cut back to no more than a couple of times a week during the winter.

Humidity: Medium. Spray it daily.

Temperature: Medium. 55 to 75 degrees.

Propagate from stem cuttings in the spring.

Earth Star

CRYPTANTHUS ACAULIS

One of the many members of the bromeliad group, the earth star looks exactly like its name—a small (no more than eight to ten inches in diameter), flattened, star-shaped rosette with stiff green leaves, often serrated, and variegated with light green or pink. Because of its striking, unusual look—almost like a gardener's starfish—and its ease of care, the earth star is a most rewarding plant for your own collection or, better yet, your children's collection.

If you do have children, I hope they have plants. Kids are perfectly capable of taking care of plants such as succulents, cacti, and bromeliads, and can be introduced to them by the time they're four or five years old. They'll love helping things grow, I promise.

Like all bromeliads, this plant will flower if it's cultivated under optimum conditions. Bright, filtered light is the key element. Spray your earth star daily to help prevent the tips from drying and turning brown—but this may happen to the lower leaves no matter what you do. When they do turn brown, simply manicure them with a sharp scissors.

"Foliar-feed" your earth star: Put a few drops of plant food into your misting water once every two weeks during the spring and summer.

SPECIFIC CARE REQUIREMENTS

Light: Bright, filtered light.
Water: Water into the cup of the plant, and make sure there's always a bit of fresh water there.
Humidity: Medium. Spray it daily.
Temperature: Medium. 50 to 75 degrees.

Propagate from offsets.

English Ivy

HEDERA HELIX

The English ivy is a very rewarding plant, either hanging in a pot or spilling out over a shelf.

There are dozens and dozens of varieties of *Hedera*—including large-leafed varieties, tiny-leafed varieties, and variegated varieties. The English ivy—which has dark green leaves with from three to five lobes—is the most common. It can be grown indoors—but disregard anything you've read that classifies this as an easy plant.

All of the varieties—including English ivy—need bright western or southern light and lots of humidity to succeed indoors.

You mustn't let this plant dry out, but you should also be very careful not to overwater. You may have to experiment with two or three plants before you find exactly how much watering they need, but a lush, healthy English ivy is well worth the trouble.

SPECIFIC CARE REQUIREMENTS

Light: Bright, filtered sunlight.
Water: Keep the soil just slightly moist.
Humidity: High. Spray this plant daily and, if it isn't hanging, keep it on a pebble tray.
Temperature: Medium. 50 to 75 degrees.

Propagate from stem cuttings.

False Aralia

DIZYGOTHECA ELEGANTISSIMA

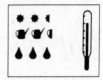

I thought I'd reached the zenith of my plant career when I learned how to *pronounce* the Latin name of this beautiful, feathery-looking plant. I knew I'd reached the zenith when I learned how to keep it flourishing indoors.

A few years ago, *People* magazine ran a picture that showed me holding a large false aralia. The editors told me that they received thousands of letters asking if I was holding a marijuana plant—and they had to reprint the picture with a clarification.

With narrow, brownish-green, leathery leaves with heavily serrated edges, the false aralia does look almost exactly like a marijuana plant.

The graceful delicacy of the false aralia is very rewarding, but giving it the proper care can be very demanding. Give it filtered eastern or southern sunlight and lots of humidity—or it will slowly lose most of its leaves, starting from the bottom up. Keep this plant out of direct sunlight, and let it just barely dry out between waterings. Humidity is the key factor in cultivating this plant—during the winter you should keep a humidifier going nearby.

Follow the care instructions below and you should be able to nurture a small false aralia into a plant that's between five and ten feet tall.

SPECIFIC CARE REQUIREMENTS

Light: Bright but indirect sunlight. Keep it out of direct sun. Filtered eastern or southern sunlight is best.

Water: Moist. Be careful not to overwater, but don't let this plant get dry for too long.

Humidity: High. Spray at least once a day.

Temperature: Warm. 65 to 85 degrees.

Propagate from stem cuttings.

False Sea Onion

ORNITHOGALUM CAUDATUM

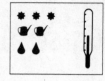

Also called the pregnant onion, climbing onion, or Zulu potato, this is a most interesting and rewarding plant. It's a succulent green bulb, grown above the soil, from which spring graceful, drooping leaves. It will also produce a cluster of little white flowers at the end of a single stem—usually two to three feet long—that emerges from the center of the plant.

If you see one, definitely, positively buy it; put it on a windowsill with bright, filtered light; keep the soil slightly moist; and then sit back and enjoy this beautiful plant.

Every now and then one of this plant's long, straplike leaves will turn brown and die. This is natural. As with most potted plants, old foliage must die to make room for the new.

The false sea onion develops little ball-like "babies" on its sides that can be potted to produce new plants. To do this, gently unpot the "mother" plant, then (carefully!), using a sharp knife or a single-edged razor blade, cut the desired babies away from the bulb. Plant them in four-inch pots with commercial potting mix.

I had a friend with literally hundreds of sea onions grown from just three mother plants. Nobody could leave her house without two or three of these plants. And then, after a few months, their friends couldn't either.

P.S. I just brought home a false sea onion that I stumbled across in a tiny plant store. I'm really excited! I'll give you an update on its progress the next time we meet.

SPECIFIC CARE REQUIREMENTS

Light: Bright, filtered light. These plants love to go outside in the shade when the temperature is above 60 degrees.
Water: Keep slightly moist.
Humidity: Medium. Spray daily.
Temperature: Medium. 55 to 75 degrees.

Propagate from offsets.

Fan Palm

CHAMAEROPS HUMILIS

The fan palm is another extremely exotic beauty—you may never have seen one because they're not all that common. But they *are* available—with a little searching. You're sure to recognize this fabulous plant when you see it: It grows up to seven feet tall on a single, reddish-brown, shaggy trunk. The tall, thin, green stalks eventually fan out like a peacock's tail—or a green Japanese fan.

Your fan palm will thrive if you keep the soil moist—which is a good rule for all palms. Too little water and the palm will dry up, too much and it will rot. So, as for all plants, try to err on the side of *under*watering—until you discover exactly how much water it takes to keep your fan palm flourishing.

This plant is most rewarding as part of a tropical motif in a bright entry hall or atrium.

SPECIFIC CARE REQUIREMENTS

Light: Filtered eastern light is perfect.
Water: Keep the soil moist, which is the rule of all palms.
Humidity: Medium. Spray it daily.
Temperature: Medium. 55 to 75 degrees.

Propagate from offsets.

Fatsia

FATSIA JAPONICA

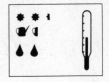

This beautiful plant—which is most often used as a large tabletop plant—is very dependable and quite easy to grow.

Its large, leathery, shiny, green leaves resemble maple leaves. These leaves, which can be anywhere from four inches to over a foot in width, grow one to a stem—and the stems can reach lengths of up to two or three feet.

Give your fatsia filtered eastern or northern light, and water it only when it's dry. The most common problem people have with fatsia is the appearance of brown spots on the leaves. This can be caused either by overwatering or by exposure to extreme temperatures.

SPECIFIC CARE REQUIREMENTS

Light: Filtered eastern light or a northern exposure would be perfect.

Water: Allow this plant to dry out, then water—but don't let it stand dry for too long.

Humidity: Medium. Mist it daily.

Temperature: Medium. 55 to 70 degrees.

Propagate by stem cuttings.

Fiddle-leaf Fig

FICUS LYRATA

A great treelike plant for a bright corner, the fiddle-leaf fig can grow to heights of ten or fifteen feet indoors. It gets its name from its large, thick, leathery, green leaves—which are shaped almost like a violin and grow straight out from the sides of a woody stem.

Like its cousins the *Ficus benjamina* (weeping fig) and *Ficus elastica decora* (India rubber tree), this is a very easy plant to grow. It requires only indirect eastern light and an occasional watering. Spray your ficus daily to help ward off brown edges on the leaves, which can be manicured with sharp scissors.

The fiddle-leaf fig makes a stunning decorative accent. Because of its height, the size and unusual shape of its leaves, and the dark, full look it has when properly tended, growing a fiddle-leaf fig is an easy way to add a lot of green to a barren corner.

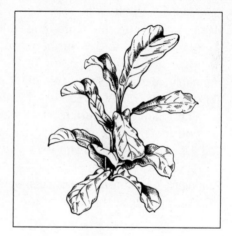

SPECIFIC CARE REQUIREMENTS

Light: Filtered light.
Water: Allow the soil to dry out between waterings. But don't wait too long!
Humidity: Medium. Spray it daily.
Temperature: Medium. 55 to 75 degrees.

Propagate from stem cuttings or by air-layering.

Fingernail Plant

NEOREGELIA SPECTABILIS

Another popular bromeliad, the fingernail plant is a tubular rosette with stiff, glossy, narrow, olive-green leaves—up to eight to ten inches long—with gray crossbands on their undersides. It gets its nickname from the red markings at the bottoms of the leaves—around the cup—and its sharp, pointed tips.

Like all bromeliads, this plant is basically ephiphytic—meaning it can derive its nourishment from the air and rain caught in its "urn"—and really doesn't need to be planted in soil. But since most of us like to keep our plants contained, use fir bark or peat moss for your planting mix.

SPECIFIC CARE REQUIREMENTS

Light: Filtered light.

Water: Water into the center cup. Allow the planting mix to dry out between waterings.

Humidity: Medium. Spray this plant daily.

Temperature: Medium. 55 to 75 degrees. This plant can tolerate more warmth if you increase the humidity.

Soil: Use fir bark or peat moss.

Propagate by planting the offsets, or "pups," that appear at the base of the plant.

Firecracker Plant

CROSSANDRA INFUNDIBULIFORMIS

This very attractive and relatively easy-to-grow flowering plant has glossy, dark green, oval leaves and produces red, orange, or pink tubular flowers that look like—you guessed it—exploded firecrackers.

Although no flowering plant is "easy" to grow, the firecracker plant comes close. I'd recommend it as a good "starter" flowering plant. Remember that success breeds confidence—and confidence is the key to growing your own green thumb.

Keep the firecracker plant in bright light and keep the soil moist. The key to caring for this plant is keeping the humidity high.

And please don't let me say "You'll get a bang out of this plant!"

SPECIFIC CARE REQUIREMENTS

Light: Bright, filtered light.
Water: Keep the soil moist.
Humidity: High. Mist your firecracker plant at least once a day and keep it on a pebble tray.
Temperature: Medium. 55 to 75 degrees.

Propagate from stem cuttings.

Flame Violet

EPISCIA *spp.*

A relative of the African violet, *Episcia* needs pretty much the same kind of extra care and attention.

Often used in hanging baskets, this tropical creeper has soft, hairy, oval leaves that range in color from green to copper with slight tinges of silver. Small red-and-yellow flowers bloom all year long, but the plant is equally prized for its spectacular foliage.

The flame violet needs bright sun (or artificial light for at least ten hours a day), moist soil, high humidity, and weekly feedings with African violet food (except during December and January). Keep your flame violet away from cold drafts—which will blacken its leaves.

SPECIFIC CARE REQUIREMENTS

Light: Bright, filtered southern sun or artificial plant lights for at least ten hours a day.

Water: Keep moist.

Humidity: High. Mist this plant at least once a day and keep it on a pebble tray.

Temperature: Warm. 65 to 85 degrees.

Propagate from offsets or leaf cuttings.

Freckle Face
or Measles Plant

HYPOESTES SANGUINOLENTA

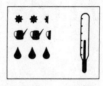

This is really a pretty little plant. Also known as the polka-dot plant, it has small, soft, oval-shaped, downy leaves spotted with rosy red markings.

Give it bright, filtered light and, most important, high humidity, and your freckle face will produce tiny lilac-colored flowers.

Although it doesn't require greenhouselike conditions, I've had good success growing the freckle face in terrariums. It also makes a great accent in a dish garden.

SPECIFIC CARE REQUIREMENTS

Light: Bright, filtered sunlight.
Water: Allow the soil to barely dry out between waterings.
Humidity: High. Spray it daily and keep it on a pebble tray.
Temperature: Medium. 55 to 75 degrees.

Propagate from stem cuttings.

Fuchsia

FUCHSIA *and cultivars*

There are dozens of varieties of fuchsia. Some are trained as standards, others make great hanging baskets. Most have medium-size green oval leaves, and all produce lots of brilliant hanging flowers—like earrings—that have a cylindrical red tube coming out of a set of slightly spreading purple or white lobes.

For maximum rewards, keep your fuchsia in bright, filtered light, keep the soil moist, and, if possible, give it a summer vacation outside—but keep it in total shade outdoors.

Fuchsias tend to suffer during the long, gray winter, so don't expect much from your plant at that time of year. Prune it back a few inches at the beginning of December, keep it away from dry heat, and allow the plant to dry out between waterings.

SPECIFIC CARE REQUIREMENTS

Light: Bright, filtered light. If outdoors, this plant must be kept in the shade.

Water: Keep the soil moist during the spring and summer, but allow it to dry out during winter.

Humidity: Medium to high. Spray the plant at least once a day, and two or three times a day during the blooming season.

Temperature: Medium. Temperatures on the cool side would be preferable.

Propagate from stem cuttings.

Gardenia

GARDENIA JASMINOIDES

This plant is also known as Cape jasmine, but to paraphrase the Bard, "a gardenia by any other name would smell as sweet." It would also be just as temperamental.

It's not that growing gardenias is difficult—they just require some very specific care in order to protect the buds and ensure flowering. Bright light and high humidity are important, but the key to culture is warmth. Cold drafts will cause the buds to drop off. It's also a good idea to give your gardenia plant an outdoor vacation—in the shade—during June, July, and August.

The best thing about gardenia plants is that, even if they never flower, their lush, dark green, shiny foliage makes them rewarding anyway. But it's just so darned frustrating when they refuse to bloom! Don't give up: Move your gardenia to a sunnier spot, water it more (unless it shows signs of overwatering—in which case water it *less*), give it more humidity, and feed it more often.

Sooner or later you'll be rewarded by the deliciously fragrant, waxy white flowers, and you'll feel even better than you did the night of your senior prom.

SPECIFIC CARE REQUIREMENTS

Light: Bright light.
Water: Keep the soil moist.
Humidity: High. Spray this plant daily and keep it on a pebble tray.
Temperature: Warm. 60 to 80 degrees.

Propagate from stem cuttings.

Geranium

PELARGONIUM *spp. and cultivars*

Once, on a radio program, I told a caller that geraniums grow like weeds. I then got an irate letter from a geranium fancier, asking how I dared to insult her beloved plants by comparing them to weeds. I tried to explain that I only meant that they're terribly easy to grow. And what's so bad about weeds, unless they're growing in your lawn or garden?

Anyway, there are hundreds of species and cultivars of geraniums. These familiar shrubby plants have fuzzy, roundish green leaves, often with interesting dark markings. They produce beautiful flowers—in a variety of colors from red to white to pink to variegated—that grow in ball-like clusters on the ends of single stems. There are also scented varieties whose leaves are absolutely delicious to squeeze and sniff.

Although geraniums like to be kept moist, overwatering will cause the leaves to turn yellow, so let the plant dry out between waterings. They bloom most profusely in spring and summer—when the days are longer and they can get more sun—but if you put in a little extra effort you can keep them blooming almost all year long.

Cut your plant back if it gets sparse and loses foliage during the winter—and keep it in a southern window during December, January, and February. During the late winter, cold nights—down to 50 degrees— will encourage it to bloom in the spring.

SPECIFIC CARE REQUIREMENTS

Light: Bright light.
Water: Drench—and then let the soil dry out
    between waterings.
Humidity: Medium. Spray this plant daily.
Temperature: Medium. 50 to 75 degrees.

Propagate from stem cuttings.

Gloxinia

SINNINGIA SPECIOSA *and cultivars*

A truly beautiful flowering plant, the gloxinia has large, dark green, velvety leaves, and produces glorious trumpet-shaped flowers in dozens of different colors. It's an especially rewarding plant because its natural blooming period is during the winter—when we need its bright flowers the most.

I say "natural" blooming period because growers have started to *force* gloxinias (and many other flowering plants) into blooming year-round. Forcing a plant to bloom means putting it through an artificially early winter—so that it blooms before it's due.

This can be a problem if you purchase a gloxinia that's blooming during the summer. Although the plant needs bright sun and likes warmth, the summer sun is usually too hot—and will melt this beautiful plant before it has a chance to perform its best.

The key to growing gloxinias is to keep them in bright light—a western or filtered southern exposure is best. Keep the soil moist, mist your plant every day with tepid water, and keep it on a pebble tray for high humidity.

The gloxinia is a distant relative of the African violet—but grows from tubers as opposed to fibrous roots. (Bulbs, tubers, and rhizomes are thick, fleshy roots that produce plants that tend to go completely dormant during certain times of the year. Fibrous-rooted plants are those with lots of stringy roots.) Therefore, your gloxinia will go completely dormant sometime during the late winter, after it finishes flowering, and its foliage will disappear. Store it in a cool, dry place for about two months, then move it out onto a sunny windowsill and begin watering it again.

SPECIFIC CARE REQUIREMENTS

Light: Bright—with a western or filtered southern exposure.
Water: Keep the soil moist.
Humidity: High. Mist this plant with tepid water daily and keep it on a pebble tray.
Temperature: Warm. 55 to 85 degrees.

Propagate from stem or leaf cuttings.

Gold-dust Tree

AUCUBA JAPONICA

I've got two of these plants, both at least four years old, and I can proudly tell you that I've never had a minute's problem with either one. They just keep growing and getting more beautiful every year.

Mine have shiny, green, oval leaves—speckled with gold dots—and have grown almost three feet tall on graceful, pliant, woody stems. Yours will too, if you keep them in bright, filtered light, water it only when the soil is dry, and spray it daily.

The gold-dust tree is often confused with *Dracaena godseffiana*, which is also green with gold speckles, but has smaller leaves and more profuse foliage.

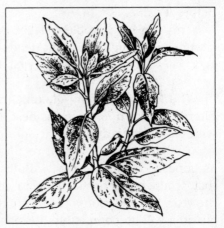

SPECIFIC CARE REQUIREMENTS

Light: Bright, filtered light.
Water: Allow the soil to dry out between waterings.
Humidity: Medium. Spray this plant daily.
Temperature: Medium. 50 to 75 degrees.

Propagate from stem cuttings.

Goldfish Plant

HYPOCYRTA NUMMULARIA

The goldfish plant isn't as easy to find as most of the plants herein, and I'm hoping its inclusion stimulates more growers and nurseries to make it available. I personally like it a lot, and I think you will too.

It's a very distinctive-looking hanging plant, with dark green, shiny leaves and beautiful bright red flowers, each of which resembles (if you stretch your imagination a bit) a goldfish.

Best of all, it's really easy to grow—for a flowering plant. That is, it needs only bright or bright, filtered light and a daily misting. Make sure to feed it weekly with a flower food during the spring and summer. It would also welcome an outdoor spring and summer vacation (in the shade).

SPECIFIC CARE REQUIREMENTS

Light: Bright, or bright, filtered light.
Water: Keep the soil moist.
Humidity: High. Spray this plant at least once a day.
Temperature: Warm. 60 to 85 degrees.

Propagate from stem cuttings.

Grape Ivy
CISSUS RHOMBIFOLIA

This is the most rewarding ivy for use in your home. It's much more dependable and just as pretty as English ivy *(Hedera helix)*, with dark green, grapelike serrated leaves growing from brownish, hairy, somewhat woody stems.

Unlike *Hedera*, which needs extraordinary light and humidity, *Cissus* will do just fine in bright, filtered light or even medium, filtered eastern or northern light—with a daily spritz.

Grape ivy, like all climbers, sends out soft, curly tendrils. It can be grown in a hanging basket, trained to climb up a pole, or even set at the base of a tall tree and allowed to climb up the trunk for a dramatic decorating effect. Grape ivy's cousin, *C. antarctica* (Kangaroo vine), is just as dependable, but has much larger, lighter green, *really* grapelike leaves.

SPECIFIC CARE REQUIREMENTS

Light: Bright, filtered light is best, although grape ivy will do fine in medium light.
Water: Allow the soil to dry out between waterings.
Humidity: Medium. Spray the plant daily.
Temperature: Medium. 50 to 75 degrees.

Propagate from stem cuttings.

Green Mexican Rose

ECHEVERIA GILVA

When you look at the large, open rosette of firm, fleshy, light green leaves, it's easy to see how this plant came by its nickname.

The green Mexican rose is not only a very interesting and beautiful plant, but, like most succulents, it's very easy to grow. The key is giving it lots of bright sunlight—and watering it only when the soil is bone dry. The plant stores a lot of water in its leaves—so be extra careful not to overwater. A sandy soil is best for this plant.

Not incidentally, if you follow these care instructions conscientiously, your green Mexican rose will reward you with a beautiful reddish-yellow flower on the end of a thin, single stem.

Another desirable variety of *Echeveria* is *E. affinis*, or black rose. This plant's leaves are darker and less fleshy than *E. gilva*'s and they sit atop thick, woody-looking stems. There are dozens of other varieties of *Echeveria*, including the popular hen and chicks, and all require the same care.

SPECIFIC CARE REQUIREMENTS

Light: Bright or bright, filtered light (at the very least).

Water: Water only when the soil is dry.

Humidity: Low. Spray this plant once a week.

Temperature: Medium. 55 to 75 degrees.

Propagate from stem cuttings.

Hawaiian Ti Plant

CORDYLINE TERMINALIS

In Hawaii I've seen ti plants grow up to fifty feet tall in the wild, and they are gorgeous. Indoors, ti plants can reach heights of eight to ten feet.

The plant's thin, leathery, sword-shaped leaves are copper-green—with distinctive red borders—and grow in a cluster on top of canelike stems. When the plant is young, the leaves are almost completely bright red.

You'll find the ti plant most rewarding if you keep it in a corner where it receives filtered eastern light. The most common problem people have with this plant is not giving it enough light—without some indirect sunlight it will lose its color. Spray your plant at least twice a day, in the morning and evening. This will help keep the tips of the leaves from turning brown.

The ti plant is sometimes also known as red dracaena. Incidentally, although some people call it the "tie" plant, I call it the "tea" plant. You may call it anything you like. Just please take care of it correctly.

SPECIFIC CARE REQUIREMENTS

Light: Filtered eastern light is best.
Water: Keep the soil slightly moist.
Humidity: Medium to high. Spray this plant at least twice a day.
Temperature: Medium. 55 to 75 degrees.

Propagate from stem cuttings.

Heliotrope

HELIOTROPIUM ARBORESCENS

This herb is a really wonderful plant from which to create a standard—because it will reach a height of four to five feet indoors. It produces large clusters of purple flowers—with an aroma reminiscent of vanilla—on top of its small, oval, wrinkled leaves.

Keep your heliotrope in filtered western or southern light and water it enough to keep the soil moist, and it should produce its fragrant blossoms from early spring through late fall. Remember to cut back on your watering during the winter months—watering only when the soil dries out.

SPECIFIC CARE REQUIREMENTS

Light: Bright, filtered light. This plant needs a filtered western or southern exposure to bloom.

Water: Keep the soil moist through the spring and summer, but allow it to dry out between waterings during the winter.

Humidity: High. Spray this plant at least once a day and keep it on a pebble tray.

Temperature: Medium. 50 to 75 degrees.

Propagate from stem cuttings.

Hibiscus
or *Chinese Hibiscus*

HIBISCUS ROSA-SINENSIS

This flowering shrub produces small, dark green, serrated leaves and large, colorful, paperlike flowers, one to a stem. Hibiscus flowers are trumpet-shaped, four or five inches wide, and very showy. Most are red, but there are also varieties with pink and with orange flowers.

Of all the flowering houseplants, hibiscus is one of the most dependable. Keep it in bright sunlight (make sure the light is slightly filtered during the heat of the summer), keep the soil damp at all times, and feed it once a month with flower food. If you follow this care conscientiously your hibiscus can bloom on and off all year long—even during the bleak winter months.

Hibiscus grows to a height of about two feet at the most, so it makes an excellent choice for a windowsill plant. Sometimes its blooms only last for a day or two, but there will always be new blooms opening to take their place.

SPECIFIC CARE REQUIREMENTS

Light: Bright sunlight—slightly filtered during the hot summer months.
Water: Keep the soil damp at all times.
Humidity: High. Mist the plant daily and keep it on a pebble tray.
Temperature: Medium. 55 to 75 degrees.

Propagate from stem cuttings.

Hyacinth

HYACINTHUS ORIENTALIS

The most important thing to know about hyacinth is that it's a one-time-only plant. Most people decide they simply must have a hyacinth when they see (or smell) it on the market each year (during December and January). This incredibly sweet-scented plant—with beautiful purple, pink, or white flowers—grows from a bulb that, generally speaking, cannot be forced to bloom in subsequent years.

Of course, there's an exception to every rule. I know of at least one person who let her hyacinth die back indoors and then planted it outside in early May. It bloomed the second spring and every year since. So you might want to try it too.

Hyacinth bulbs can be purchased during late winter and planted in a pot of soil, or just set on a pebble tray filled with water. They will bloom in about two to three weeks, first producing foliage and then large clusters of flowers on six-inch-tall stems. To keep them in bloom for the longest possible time (which is about three weeks), follow the instructions below.

SPECIFIC CARE REQUIREMENTS

Light: Bright light.

Water: Keep the soil moist at all times, or make sure the pebble tray is full of water.

Humidity: No misting is necessary.

Temperature: Medium. 55 to 75 degrees.

Propagate from new bulbs.

India Rubber Tree

FICUS ELASTICA, *also* F. ELASTICA DECORA
(broad-leaf India rubber tree)

No, rubber is no longer made from this plant, and contained in a pot it will never stretch to a height of one hundred feet like its wild counterparts, but who do you know with hundred-foot ceilings? (Rubber, by the way, is now made from *Hevea braziliensis*, which will *not* grow indoors.) This plant can, however, reach heights of ten to twelve feet indoors, and its sap is white and sticky and very much like that of the true rubber tree.

The India rubber tree has large, oblong, thick, shiny, dark, olive-green, leathery leaves (whew!) that emerge from the top of the plant out of red, tubular sheaths.

I've gotten lots of complaints from rubber tree owners that they've completely lost at least one, and sometimes two, of the three stalks that are usually potted together. My theory is that most rubber trees are raised outdoors under lath, instead of in greenhouses, and simply find the transition to house or apartment conditions too severe. My solution—give this plant lots and lots of humidity.

SPECIFIC CARE REQUIREMENTS

Light: Bright, filtered light.
Water: Keep the soil just slightly moist.
Humidity: High. Spray the plant daily and keep it on a pebble tray.
Temperature: Medium. 55 to 75 degrees.

Propagate from stem cuttings.

Irish Lace Fern

NEPHROLEPSIS EXALTATA *"verona"*

If I were backed up against the garden wall and forced to pick my very favorite plant, I suspect it would be the Irish lace fern. Beauty is in the eye of the beholder, of course, but I think you'll love the look of this plant too.

It's technically a dwarf variety of Boston fern, except that its light green fronds are much finer and lacier and far more delicate. The plant grows in a tight, lush, dense manner that completely hides the soil and just begs you to reach out and stroke it. And it's best that you do, because the Irish lace fern is among the most challenging plants in this book.

Frankly, Irish lace fern is very difficult to grow outside a greenhouse. But when you succeed—as I did after five tries—you'll feel the same exhilaration I did. I know five tries may seem excessive, and you probably won't run into five Irish lace ferns in your life—but when I get determined, I get *obsessed*.

What is my formula for success? After failing twice while trying to grow the plant in a terrarium, where it rotted for want of air, and twice more with plants in an eastern exposure, I finally tried to grow an Irish lace fern in a northern window.

I placed the plant on a pebble tray and set up a small humidifier—which I kept on almost constantly—about four feet away. I watered the plant from the bottom, sitting the plant, in its clay pot, in a couple of inches of water until all the water had been sucked up into the roots. (This keeps the soil moist and helps avoid crown rot.) I also added food to the water about once a month.

The result has been a successful run of almost three years—and probably the most rewarding plant experience I've ever had!

SPECIFIC CARE REQUIREMENTS

Light: Medium to low. A northern window is just right.

Water: Keep the soil moist. Water the plant from below.

Humidity: Keep it on a pebble tray and near a humidifier.

Temperature: Medium. 55 to 70 degrees. Avoid extreme heat and cold drafts.

Propagate by division.

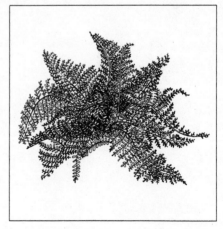

Irish Moss
or *Spike Moss*

SELAGINELLA *spp.*

Because it thrives in low light and needs lots of humidity, Irish moss really should be kept in a terrarium. With its beautiful mosslike cushions of densely clustered, emerald-green branches, this plant makes a perfect ground cover in any glass garden.

Unless you keep the humidity as high as possible, the plant will quickly dry out—and you'll be stuck with a pot full of yellow, dry, dead moss.

There are a couple of other species of *Selaginella* commercially available, especially *S. emmeliana*, which has a fernlike appearance and is also a good terrarium candidate.

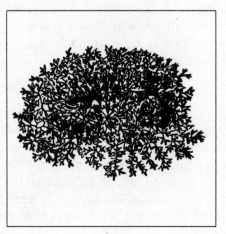

SPECIFIC CARE REQUIREMENTS

Light: Low. This plant prefers a shady location.
Water: Keep the soil moist.
Humidity: High. Keep this plant in a terrarium.
Temperature: Warm. 60 to 85 degrees.

Propagate from stem cuttings.

Jade Plant

CRASSULA ARGENTEA

This very familiar branching succulent has thick, fleshy, shiny, dark green leaves—which are rounded on the top and flat on the bottom. These leaves tend to turn reddish in the sun, which is natural and nothing to be concerned about. Kept in good bright sun, the jade plant will produce lots of small, pinkish-white flowers.

The complaint I hear most often about the jade plant is that the lower leaves are falling off. This means that the plant's not getting enough light. You should also keep your eyes on the leaves, which should be firm and round. If they're not getting enough water, they'll begin to wrinkle up and flatten out.

SPECIFIC CARE REQUIREMENTS

Light: Bright sun. This plant can stand a really bright southern exposure.

Water: Medium. Allow the soil to dry out thoroughly between waterings.

Humidity: Low. Spray it once a week.

Temperature: Medium. 55 to 75 degrees.

Propagate from stem cuttings.

Jasmine

CESTRUM NOCTURNUM

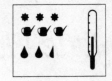

The jasmine is a very dependable flowering plant—compared, for instance, to its temperamental cousin, the gardenia. It's a bushy, vining, dark green shrub that grows very quickly and produces white, star-shaped, extremely fragrant flowers. The variety *Cestrum nocturnum* is the famous night-blooming jasmine—whose flowers take on a much heavier aroma at night.

Jasmine is not as difficult to grow as most flowering plants. Just hang it in an eastern window and water it frequently enough to keep the soil moist.

The foliage will almost always stay healthy, especially if you cut it back three or four inches every spring. The biggest problem is finding just the right combination of care to coax the plant into bloom. If you want your jasmine to bloom, you'll have to experiment with variations on the specific care requirements that follow.

SPECIFIC CARE REQUIREMENTS

Light: Bright, filtered light.
Water: Keep the soil moist.
Humidity: Medium. Spray this plant daily.
Temperature: Medium. 55 to 75 degrees.

Propagate from stem cuttings.

Kafir Lily
CLIVIA MINIATA

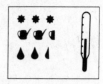

This is a beautiful flowering bulb plant with long, straplike, arching leaves and large, orange, bell-shaped flowers. The flowers grow in clusters at the end of a tall, thick stalk—which can grow up to two feet high.

Give your Kafir lily an eastern or filtered southern exposure, and let the soil dry out between waterings—and it will bloom every year from late winter through summer.

After the flowers die, let the plant rest in an unheated room through the fall and winter—with no food and just enough water to keep the leaves from drooping. In March, bring it back into a sunny location and begin regular watering and feeding. New blossoms will soon emerge.

SPECIFIC CARE REQUIREMENTS

Light: Bright, filtered light.

Water: When it's in bloom, water this plant thoroughly, then let it dry out before the next watering. During dormancy, water it no more than a couple of times a month.

Humidity: Medium. Spray this plant daily during the blooming season.

Temperature: Medium (during the blooming season). 55 to 75 degrees.

Propagate by division.

Kentia Palm

HOWEIA FORSTERIANA

Several palms will do very well indoors—given the proper light. My favorite among these tropical beauties is the kentia palm *(Howeia forsteriana)*.

Usually sold with four stalks to the pot, the kentia can grow up to ten to fifteen feet tall indoors. You've probably seen it in shady corners of truly elegant hotel lobbies. Its tough, dark-green pinnate leaves, on thick, graceful fronds, make it a striking addition to any decor.

Keep your kentia palm potbound, as it tends to die back when transplanted into too large a container. Make sure it's in a location where it will get no more than filtered eastern light, and be sure to keep the soil moist.

Caveat Emptor: Beware of the *Areca*, or betel nut palm. This tree has dense, erect, light green, feathery foliage and is usually very inexpensive. For example, a ten-foot-tall areca palm might cost around $25.00, while a ten-foot-tall kentia palm could cost as much as $125.00. The kentia will survive for years and years, while the areca will have problems surviving more than a few months—at the most—indoors.

SPECIFIC CARE REQUIREMENTS

Light: Preferably filtered eastern light, but a northern exposure will be fine.
Water: Keep the soil slightly moist.
Humidity: Medium. Mist this plant daily.
Temperature: Medium. 55 to 70 degrees.

Propagate from seeds or offsets.

Lipstick Plant

AESCHYNANTHUS JAVANICUS

This attractive hanging vine has small, oval, dark green leaves. Bright red tubular flowers—that resemble a lipstick—appear on the ends of its vines.

The lipstick plant will grow best if you keep it in bright, filtered sunlight and water it often enough to keep the soil moist. It will flower from late spring through late summer. Feed it twice a month during this period, but do not feed it during the fall and winter. It would love an outdoor vacation—in the shade—starting in late spring and continuing through the summer.

Though not hard to grow, the lipstick plant will lose lots of leaves from the top of its stems—around the plant's crown—if not properly cared for.

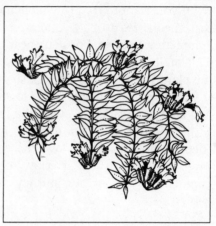

SPECIFIC CARE REQUIREMENTS

Light: Bright, filtered light.
Water: Keep the soil moist.
Humidity: Medium. Spray this plant daily.
Temperature: Medium. 55 to 75 degrees.

Propagate from stem cuttings.

Living Rocks

LITHOPS *spp.*

Living rocks are flat or round-topped succulents that are part of one of the most fascinating groups in the plant kingdom. There are dozens of varieties, but they all look remarkably like rocks. I've seen *Lithops* arranged with real rocks so that only the closest inspection will reveal which are the "dead" rocks and which are the living ones.

Caring for these "living rocks" is simple—give them bright sunlight and water them only when the soil is bone dry.

If you want to try growing living rocks, check your Yellow Pages for a nursery that specializes in cacti and succulents. They are sometimes available at large, complete nurseries, but your best bet is the specialist.

You'll probably find lots of them flowering—a white flower, often larger than the plant itself, emerging on a single stem from a split in the middle of the plant. If you want *your* living rocks to flower, give them optimum growing conditions and cool winter nights—with the temperature around 50 degrees.

Lithops are great fun to grow, and your collection will delight and amaze your friends. Kids especially love these plants, and, because they need only minimal care, they're a perfect way to start a young'un on his or her journey down the garden path.

SPECIFIC CARE REQUIREMENTS

Light: Bright sunlight.
Water: Allow the soil to dry out completely
between waterings.
Humidity: Low. Spray this plant once a
week.
Temperature: Medium. 50 to 75 degrees.

Propagate from offsets.

Maidenhair Fern

ADIANTUM RADDIANUM

It's almost impossible to resist buying this plant. Arguably the most beautiful of all the ferns—because of its dark green fronds; dainty, feather-formed leaves; and extraordinarily lacy lushness—the soft, delicate maidenhair fern *must* go into a terrarium.

Like most ferns, the maidenhair fern requires very special care: Keep it in a terrarium where it gets no more than filtered eastern light (although a northern exposure is preferable), keep the soil moist, and, most important, keep the humidity as high as possible. Even if it's in a terrarium, you'll have to spray this plant at least twice a day.

Be warned that unless you provide the plant with the optimum, almost greenhouse conditions that I've described your maidenhair fern will be just a potful of brown, organic crepe paper within a few weeks.

SPECIFIC CARE REQUIREMENTS

Light: Indirect, filtered light.
Water: Keep the soil moist.
Humidity: High. Keep this plant in a terrarium and spray it twice a day.
Temperature: Medium to warm. Cold drafts can do your maidenhair fern in quickly.

Propagate by division.

Mango

MANGIFERA INDICA

This is another plant that you can grow from the contents of your grocery bag. If you're successful, the flat, oval mango pit will develop into a lovely indoor tree—with sword-shaped, slightly serrated leaves. It will make a wonderful addition to your indoor decor—either on a windowsill or in a bright corner.

Cultivating this plant can be a lot of fun: First, let the mango pit dry out. Then plant it—horizontally—in regular potting mix in a six-inch pot. Keep the pot in the sun and the soil moist, and within two or three weeks you'll be rewarded with clusters of leaves that start out almost red, then, as they mature, turn apricot, then light green, and finally dark green in color. Your mango tree can grow up to six or seven feet tall indoors, and might even bear fruit after four or five years.

Besides bright sun and moist soil, the real key to success with this plant is high humidity—unless it's sprayed at least twice a day the leaves, especially the lower ones, will dry up and fall off.

SPECIFIC CARE REQUIREMENTS

Light: Bright or bright, filtered light at the very least.
Water: Keep the soil moist.
Humidity: Medium. Spray this plant daily.
Temperature: Medium. 55 to 75 degrees.

Propagate from stem cuttings or seeds.

Ming Aralia

POLYSCIAS FRUTICOSA

I think that the Ming aralia is one of the most beautiful foliage plants in the world. Dark green, somewhat curly, leathery, feathery leaves grow in clusters on willowy branches that are attached to a thick, treelike stem.

It's difficult to find exactly the right spot for this fairly challenging plant—the key to success is making sure it gets proper light and humidity.

Make sure your Ming aralia gets plenty of bright light. Lower leaf drop is a major concern—if the plant gets too little light, the leaves will quickly turn yellow and drop off. It also needs *lots* of humidity. Spray the plant frequently, or keep it near a humidifier.

If you follow the care instructions conscientiously you'll be rewarded with a beautiful, long-lasting plant.

SPECIFIC CARE REQUIREMENTS

Light: Bright light is vital to this plant.
Water: Keep the soil slightly moist at all times.
Humidity: High. Spray this plant frequently.
Temperature: Medium. 55 to 75 degrees.

Propagate from stem cuttings.

Miracle Leaf Plant

KALANCHOE BLOSSFELDIANA

This very dependable blooming succulent earns its nickname by producing young plantlets, seemingly miraculously, from the centers of its green, scalloped leaves. It will also bear large clusters of tiny red, yellow, or pink flowers, especially during the winter months. Thus another nickname, the Christmas kalanchoe.

It doesn't take a miracle to keep the miracle leaf plant thriving and flourishing. In fact, it takes practically no effort at all. Just keep it in bright, filtered light and let it dry out between waterings. Like all succulents, this plant stores water in its leaves.

To help force your kalanchoe into its "Christmas" blooming, restrict its exposure to light so that it gets long, dark nights. I recommend "lights out" between 6 P.M. and 7 A.M.

Just one of dozens of species of kalanchoes, the miracle leaf plant is most rewarding as part of a collection of succulents. Some other interesting kalanchoes you may want to try include the panda plant (*K. tomentosa*, page 112), or the air plant (*K. pinnata*).

SPECIFIC CARE REQUIREMENTS

Light: Bright. A filtered or slightly indirect southern exposure would be ideal.

Water: Allow the soil to dry out between waterings.

Humidity: Low. Spray this plant once a week.

Temperature: Medium. 55 to 75 degrees.

Propagate from stem cuttings.

Mosaic Plant or Nerve Plant

FITTONIA VERSCHAFFELTII
or F. verschaffeltii argyoneura

Grown for its striking foliage, the mosaic plant is a low-growing, creeping herb. Its stems are filled with small, bright green, papery leaves that are spectacularly webbed with white or deep pink veins.

The nerve plant might make you nervous, because even if you care for it properly—giving it filtered eastern light, keeping the soil moist, and spraying it daily—it's not an easy plant to grow. You'll need to work out exactly the right combination of light, water, and humidity—or it will become leggy and straggly, or just dry up and die.

It can do very well, however, in a terrarium. Just make sure to pinch the plant back when it gets straggly.

While its unusual beauty can be immensely rewarding, the mosaic plant helps prove the old plant adage: "If it looks delicate, it probably is." (Actually, I just made that up—but it seems to be true.)

SPECIFIC CARE REQUIREMENTS

Light: Medium light or shady locations. Filtered eastern light or northern light is perfect.

Water: Keep the soil moist.

Humidity: Medium to high. Spray this plant at least once a day and keep it on a pebble tray. Or, better yet, keep this plant in a terrarium.

Temperature: Medium. 55 to 75 degrees.

Propagate from stem cuttings.

Moses-in-the-cradle

RHOEO DISCOLOR

Moses-in-the-cradle gets its name from the way its little white flower clusters grow down in the center of its boat-shaped rosette.

Give it bright, filtered light—and water it once a week during the winter (and twice a week during the summer)—and your *Rhoeo* will grow into a rosette of stiff, waxy, lance-shaped leaves that are dark green on top and bright purple on the undersides. The Moses-in-the-cradle is a very easy plant to grow, and a most interesting one to add to your collection.

SPECIFIC CARE REQUIREMENTS

Light: Bright, filtered light.
Water: Keep the soil moist.
Humidity: Medium. Spray this plant daily.
Temperature: Medium. Between 55 and 75 degrees.

Propagate by division.

Natal Plum

CARISSA GRANDIFLORA

The natal plum is a spectacular plant, especially when bearing its edible, scarlet, plumlike fruit. It is a woody shrub that has lustrous, green, oval leaves and produces large white flowers (which precede the fruit). Beware of the sharp spines on the stems!

It can reach a height of three to four feet indoors, as long as you give it bright sun (in a western or southern exposure) and keep the soil moist.

There is a thornless variety—*C. grandiflora nana*—but I haven't had the same success at coaxing this variety into producing fruit. Another excellent variety, *C. spectabilis* (commonly known as wintersweet), has narrower leaves than *C. grandiflora* and pure white flowers with a much more pronounced and delightful scent, but it is difficult to find.

SPECIFIC CARE REQUIREMENTS

Light: Bright light. A western or southern exposure is best.

Water: Keep the soil moist.

Humidity: High. Spray this plant at least once a day during the spring and summer, and keep it on a "dry well," or pebble tray.

Temperature: Medium. 55 to 75 degrees.

Propagate from stem cuttings.

Neanthe Bella Palm or *Dwarf Palm*

CHAMAEDOREA ELEGANS

This terrific plant is one of my very favorites. Although it's often called a parlor palm, I've got one in my bedroom. I've raised it from a seedling into a full, lush, symmetrical beauty that has reached the maximum height for this plant—about three feet.

Although it's not a spectacular plant, the *Neanthe bella* palm is quite attractive and ideal for shady locations. It grows slowly, with slim stems bearing thin, pinnate, leathery leaves. In brighter light it will produce stalklike flowers that look like rows of yellow seeds on a stem, but that's strictly a bonus.

Although this plant prefers more light to less, it can do remarkably well in a shady location. And by the way—keep your dwarf palm potbound for best results.

SPECIFIC CARE REQUIREMENTS

Light: Medium to low light.
Water: Keep the soil damp.
Humidity: Medium. Spray this plant daily.
Temperature: Medium. 55 to 75 degrees.

Propagate from seeds.

Norfolk Island Pine
or *Star Pine*

ARAUCARIA HETEROPHYLLA

Even though this native of Norfolk Island, Australia, isn't really a pine, the nick-name "star pine" is most appropriate.

Its branches have needles like those on a pine tree and branch out in a star shape from a woody trunk. It looks very much like the traditional Christmas tree, starting with wide branches at the bottom and getting narrower toward the top. In fact, I know lots of people who decorate their star pines during the holiday season and save a ton of money by not having to buy a temporary tree.

In its native habitat the star pine can reach heights of up to a hundred feet, but indoors they range anywhere from a few inches to about six feet tall.

I find this a very easy plant to grow under the right conditions. The key is to give the star pine bright, filtered sunlight, moist soil, and a daily misting. If any of these conditions is missing, the star pine will lose lots of lower branches—which will turn yellow and fall off.

SPECIFIC CARE REQUIREMENTS

Light: Bright, filtered light. This plant will suffer in a shady location.
Water: Keep the soil slightly moist.
Humidity: Medium. Spray this plant daily.
Temperature: Medium. 55 to 75 degrees.

Propagate from stem cuttings.

Old Man Cactus

CEPHALOCEREUS SENILIS

Of all the hundreds of varieties of cacti, the old man cactus never fails to catch the buyer's eye. Its appearance is very unusual: a slender column covered with long, white or gray hairs.

Caring for this plant—and all cacti—is easy. Basically, these very hardy plants have been forced to adapt to the extreme conditions of their native desert. They like bright—even hot—sun during the day, but can tolerate cool, cool, nights.

Water cacti only when the soil is completely dry. And, speaking of soil, use a mixture of one-half commercial potting mix and one-half sand. Feed your old man cactus once every two weeks—during the spring and summer—with a commercial cactus food.

If you want to get your cactus to bloom indoors during the spring and summer, see that it gets long, cool (40 degrees) nights during the winter. And if the new growth at the top gets thin and somewhat splindly, give the plant more light and start feeding it once a week. Don't worry, you'll never have to take it in for a haircut.

SPECIFIC CARE REQUIREMENTS

Light: Bright light.
Water: Allow the soil to dry out thoroughly between waterings.
Humidity: Low. Spray once a week at most.
Temperature: Medium. 55 to 75 degrees.

Propagate from stem cuttings or seeds.

Orchid

CATTLEYA *spp.*

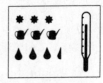

Popular mythology says that orchids are delicate and difficult and out of the reach of the average indoor gardener. That's just a myth. Although many varieties of orchid do need greenhouse conditions, many others will do very well in your house or apartment—if you know which varieties to buy and how to care for them.

One of the best choices for the beginning orchid grower is the *Cattleya* orchid. There are more than fifty species of *Cattleya*, and thousands of varieties and hybrids, but all will thrive in your home as long as you provide lots of sunlight (western or southern is best) and high humidity. The foliage will survive less light, but the blooms will be sparse.

Cattleyas, like most orchids, must be grown in osmunda or fir bark as opposed to soil, and will do best if their roots are kept potbound.

Proper temperature is important—temperatures should range from 55 degrees at night up to 75 degrees during the day. On very hot days, spray the plant often, as too much heat will do the plant in.

Watering *Cattleya* orchids is a bit tricky and perhaps the key factor to successful cultivation. During the summer, water frequently so that the fir bark or osmunda is always moist. During the winter, let the plant dry out completely between waterings.

Feed *Cattleyas* with a commercial orchid food—twice a month during the summer, once a month during the fall, and not at all during the winter months.

Other orchid varieties that will do well indoors include *Cymbidium*, *Phalaenopsis*, *Vanda*, and *Paphiopedilum* (or lady's slipper).

Given proper sunlight, watering, and humidity, all of these plants will reward you with flowers—varying in size from miniature up to six inches across, and bursting forth in an infinite variety of colors and patterns.

Since even small, starter orchid plants are expensive, you should really prepare yourself thoroughly before starting down this particular garden path. Get and read a book that deals solely with the care and feeding of orchids. See if there's an orchid society in your city. Learn as much as you can. And be prepared to have a few failures—as you learn how to provide the perfect care and feeding for this most rewarding houseplant.

Then get growing, and see if you—like a friend of mine—can have over a hundred orchid plants blooming on *your* windowsill.

SPECIFIC CARE REQUIREMENTS

Light: Bright, bright filtered light.
Water: Keep the potting mix moist.
Humidity: High. Spray the plant daily and
   keep it on a pebble tray.
Temperature: Medium. 55 to 75 degrees.
   Temperature must *never* drop below 55.

Propagate by division.

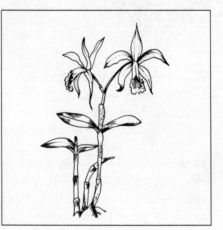

Panda Plant

KALANCHOE TOMENTOSA

I really like this plant, and I'll bet you'll find it irresistible. Its soft, fleshy, spoon-shaped leaves are covered with what feels and looks exactly like white velvet. You almost want to cuddle it!

Like all succulents, it's very easy to care for. Give it lots of bright light and very little water—let the soil dry out completely between waterings.

Since the panda plant comes in an infinite number of spectacular forms and shapes, it's a must for succulent collectors and another plant that the kids will love.

SPECIFIC CARE REQUIREMENTS

Light: Bright sunlight.
Water: Water only when the soil is dry.
Humidity: Low. Spray this plant once a
   week.
Temperature: Medium. 55 to 75 degrees.

Propagate from stem cuttings.

Peacock Plant

CALATHEA MAKOYANA

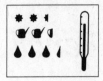

The peacock plant is related to the prayer plant (same family—*Marantaceae*) and has equally colorful markings. Each oval leaf, which can grow up to five feet long, has a delicate design of olive-green lines and circles on a background of pale green. The same pattern, in purple, can be found on the underside of the leaf.

The peacock plant doesn't need or want much light. In fact, too much direct, bright light will burn the plant right up. Without enough humidity, though, the leaves will turn yellow at the edges and then curl up and die. Beware of cold drafts, which can kill a *Calathea*.

Because of its beauty, the peacock plant can be very rewarding, but it's difficult to grow outside of a greenhouse or terrarium. You will be proud as a peacock if you succeed.

SPECIFIC CARE REQUIREMENTS

Light: Medium. Filtered light is essential.
Water: Keep the soil moist.
Humidity: High. Spray this plant daily and keep it on a pebble tray or in a terrarium.
Temperature: Warm. 65 to 80 degrees.

Propagate from stem cuttings and by division.

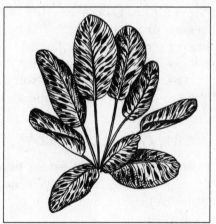

Pencil Tree

EUPHORBIA TIRUCALLI

I love the unique appearance of this succulent, but beware: It's full of a milklike sap that's relatively poisonous. If you add this plant to your collection, be sure to take all the necessary precautions to keep it out of the reach of small children and plant-eating animals.

Having warned you of this danger, let me encourage you to try this plant if you can find it. You'll recognize the pencil tree at once: It's a treelike plant with smooth, glossy, green, cylindrical branches that are approximately as thick as a pencil growing out from a much thicker trunk. A great specimen looks like a tree with lots and lots of branches and no leaves. It can grow from a couple of feet up to thirty feet tall in its natural habitat.

As for most succulents, the pencil tree is easy to care for. Give it lots of bright western or southern light, and water it only when the soil dries out. Not enough sun, or too much water, and the lead will quickly go out of your pencil tree—it will get mushy, droop, and then die.

The pencil tree is also sold commercially as the milk plant, or the stick plant.

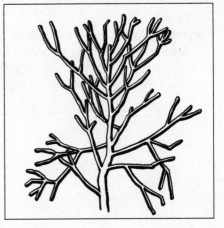

SPECIFIC CARE REQUIREMENTS

Light: Bright light. A western or southern exposure—as for all succulents.

Water: Allow the soil to dry out between waterings.

Humidity: Low. Spray this plant once a week.

Temperature: Medium. 50 to 75 degrees.

Propagate from stem cuttings.

Peperomia

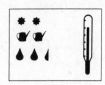

Peperomias are low-growing plants that look great on a tabletop. You'll see three or four different species of this most interesting and rewarding plant. The most common is *Peperomia obtusifolia*, which has succulent stems and waxy, green, oval leaves up to two to three inches wide, which are sometimes splashed with yellow. *P. caperata* (shown), or Emerald Ripple peperomia, has smaller, round, dark green leaves that are wrinkled like a water-sodden finger. The other commonly available variety is *P. sandersii* (var. *argyreia*), the watermelon peperomia, named for its grayish-green, oval leaves marked with vertical silver lines.

Care for all peperomias is the same: Give them filtered, indirect light, and, most important, let them dry out between waterings. These plants have extremely succulent stems, and the most common problem—mushy, rotting stems—is caused by overwatering.

By the way, I can't begin to count the number of telephone calls and letters I've gotten over the years that began by proclaiming, "Mr. Mother Earth, I've got a terrible problem with my pepperoni." I patiently explain you can only have a problem with pepperoni on a pizza. The name of the plant is *peperomia*.

SPECIFIC CARE REQUIREMENTS

Light: Filtered, indirect light.
Water: Allow the soil to dry out between waterings.
Humidity: Medium. Mist this plant daily.
Temperature: Warm. 65 to 85 degrees.

Propagate from stem or leaf cuttings or by division.

Philodendron

PHILODENDRON *spp.*

Since I begin every book, television appearance, and radio show with, "Hi there, philodendron phans!" it would be unthinkable for me not to include a few philodendrons among my Most Rewarding Houseplants.

Why did I choose this particular species as my signature plant? Back in the beginning, nearly twenty years ago, the philodendron was practically the only species of houseplant (besides palms and ferns) that you could buy. Most people thought that every plant was a philodendron—and they weren't far wrong!

There are hundreds of varieties of philodendron—far too many to list separately—but that's what makes them so rewarding. There's such a variety of different shapes, sizes, and colors that you could grow a hundred different kinds of philodendron and no one would know that they weren't a hundred different plants. They're also easy to care for and great for low-light situations.

The most common philodendrons: *P. cordatum*, or heart-leaf philodendron, is a vining variety with darkish-green, heart-shaped leaves. You'll see it either cascading over the sides of a hanging pot or crawling up a board or pole as a floor plant. *P. rubrum*, an erect variety, has wide, shiny, deep reddish-green leaves. *P. hastatum*, another erect variety, has leathery green leaves shaped like a thin elephant's ear. And *P. lyrata*, a vining variety, has shiny green leaves shaped enough like a violin that it's nicknamed the "fiddle-leaf" philodendron.

All philodendrons need no more than indirect light and should be watered only when the soil dries out.

The most common problem you'll have with this most dependable plant is that its new growth will come in smaller and smaller. To correct this condition, give your philodendrons more sunlight, and don't forget to feed them at least once a month during the spring and summer.

SPECIFIC CARE REQUIREMENTS

Light: Medium to low. A northern exposure is fine for any variety of philodendron.
Water: Let the soil dry out between waterings.
Humidity: Medium. Spray your plant daily.
Temperature: Medium. Between 50 and 70 degrees.

Propagate from stem cuttings.

Piggyback Plant

TOLMIEA MENZIESII

This low-growing, bushy plant has hairy, soft, light green, serrated leaves and is somewhat temperamental. It's nickname refers to its habit of sprouting new leaves right out of the middle of its old leaves.

The piggyback plant needs bright, filtered light to produce its plantlets. The plant will survive in a shadier location, but won't produce the profusion of dramatic plantlets that make it so much fun to grow.

But the most important element is lots of water. If you let the piggyback dry out, it will droop completely and appear to be dead. It isn't. A good drink will revive it. Water it thoroughly, place it in a bright spot, and it will "come back to life" in an hour or so. But don't let this happen too often—the plant will eventually fail to recover.

Make sure you put a layer of plastic wrap or aluminum foil around the rim of the piggyback's pot. The stems of this plant are very sensitive to the salts that accumulate (from the soil and the water) on the pot—and stems that touch the rim will turn brown and die.

SPECIFIC CARE REQUIREMENTS

Light: Bright, filtered light.
Water: Keep soil moist at all times.
Humidity: Medium. Spray daily with tepid water.
Temperature: Medium. 55 to 75 degrees.

Propagate by planting plantlets.

Pineapple

ANANUS COMOSUS

The pineapple is easily the most recognizable of all the bromeliads. You can grow a pineapple plant simply by twisting the top off a store-bought pineapple and planting it in soil.

Keep your pineapple plant in bright light and keep fresh water in the center of the rosette (that will form in about three to four weeks). The rosette will be about six inches across, and it will be gray-green, stiff, and have spiny-edged leaves.

If you want the plant to flower—and who doesn't?—cut an apple in half, put half of the apple into the "urn" of the plant, and cover it with an airtight plastic bag. The ethlyene gas the apple gives off will help stimulate the pineapple to flower. (See also the urn plant, page 139.)

Other commercially available varieties include *A. variegatus*, which has large, creamy stripes and pinkish tones on its leaves, and *A. nanus*, a miniature species that bears small, pinkish fruit.

Although your pineapple plant will flourish with minimum care, it's highly unlikely to bear fruit in your home—unless you live in a field in Hawaii.

SPECIFIC CARE REQUIREMENTS

Light: Bright light.

Water: Keep the soil slightly moist and keep fresh water in the center of the rosette.

Humidity: High. Spray this plant at least once a day to keep the leaves from drying out and dying.

Temperature: Medium. 55 to 75 degrees.

Propagate from offshoots.

Poinsettia

EUPHORBIA PULCHERRIMA

This traditional Christmas flowering plant is easy to maintain. When you first bring it home—fresh and in full, glorious bloom—it needs only bright light and watering when dry. It's getting it to rebloom that can be a hassle.

Your poinsettia will have papery, light green, lobed, ovate leaves with red, white, or pink bracts at the top. These are *not* the flowers! Bracts are leaflike plant parts that are right near the flower and are usually thought (wrongly) to be petals. The real flowers are those tiny little yellow fellows growing in a cluster at the top of each stem.

If you want your poinsettia to rebloom each winter, put it into total darkness (such as a closet) for ten to twelve hours every night for at least eight weeks in a row—starting around the beginning of October.

Don't forget to bring it out into a sunny window each day before repeating the "blackout" process each night.

Better yet, just prune it back after it finishes flowering (and the leaves turn yellow, dry up, and fall off), and enjoy it as a foliage plant for years and years.

SPECIFIC CARE REQUIREMENTS

Light: Bright, or bright, filtered light. The more light the better while the bracts are still colorful.

Water: Allow the soil to dry out between waterings. But don't let it stay dry too long.

Humidity: Medium to high. Spray this plant daily if you're maintaining it as a foliage plant.

Temperature: Medium. 55 to 75 degrees.

Propagate from stem cuttings.

Ponytail Palm
or Bottle Palm

BEAUCARNEA RECURVATA

This isn't really a palm, but is a member of the *Agave* family. The treelike plant has a round, woody, swollen base—from which a rosette of thin, rough, green leaves emerges. These leaves will grow long and then droop gracefully.

It's very easy to grow and can make a spectacular decorative display in a bright, southern corner.

The fascinating thing about the *Beaucarnea* is that it can store up to a year's worth of water—depending on its size—in its bulbous base. This astonishing capacity makes it a most rewarding choice for people who are out of town a lot.

And I've often wondered why "camel plant" hasn't been added to its list of nicknames.

SPECIFIC CARE REQUIREMENTS

Light: Bright light. This plant can even take a southern exposure.

Water: Allow the soil to dry thoroughly between waterings. The ponytail palm can go weeks without water.

Humidity: Low. Mist your plant once a week.

Temperature: Medium. 50 to 75 degrees.

Propagate from offsets.

Prayer Plant

MARANTA LEUCONEURA

This beautiful, delicate, low-growing plant has paper-thin, dark green, oval leaves splotched with deep brown spots. The leaves of another common variety are streaked with red. Because of these distinctive markings, the prayer plant is sometimes called "rabbit tracks." If properly cared for, this plant can produce tiny white flowers.

The prayer plant is a great favorite with indoor gardeners, especially kids, because of its habit of folding its leaves upward at night—as if in prayer. In its native habitat, this helps the plant store moisture to quench its thirst during the night.

Although this plant is fun to grow and lovely to look at, it can be somewhat difficult. The most common problem is for the leaf edges to dry out and turn brown or yellow. This typically happens soon after you bring the plant home. You can try to correct this problem by spraying the plant more often and by decreasing the amount of light it's getting.

Besides watering, feeding, and spraying, it might help to toss in a prayer from time to time.

SPECIFIC CARE REQUIREMENTS

Light: Filtered light. Bright, hot sun will burn this plant to a crisp in a hurry.

Water: Keep the soil slightly moist.

Humidity: High. Mist your plant daily and keep it on a pebble tray.

Temperature: Medium. 55 to 75 degrees. If the plant is getting lots and lots of humidity it can stand higher temperatures.

Propagate from stem cuttings.

Purple Velvet

GYNURA AURANTIACA

A most beautiful hanging plant, purple velvet has fleshy, dark green, almost iridescent leaves covered with velvety purple hairs. This plant is often confused with *G. sarmentosa*, or purple passion plant, because the two look almost identical.

Proper care is the same for both purple plants: Give them both bright, or at least bright, filtered light and enough water to keep the soil moist. Pinching new growth off frequently is the key to keeping this plant full and bushy.

You should spray your purple velvet daily—but make sure you use tepid water in your spray bottle. All hairy-leafed plants, such as African violet, piggyback, and purple velvet tend to develop leaf spots if sprayed with cold water.

One caution about this plant: Properly cultivated, it will produce clusters of tiny orange flowers that should be pinched off as soon as they appear—they have a very unpleasant odor. You'll know when your purple velvet plant has sprung into bloom. Just follow your nose.

SPECIFIC CARE REQUIREMENTS

Light: Bright, or at the very least bright, filtered light.
Water: Keep the soil moist.
Humidity: Medium. Spray this plant daily with *tepid* water.
Temperature: Medium. 55 to 75 degrees.

Propagate from stem cuttings.

Purple Waffle Plant

HEMIGRAPHIS *ssp.*

"I've never seen a purple cow. . . ." Well, I never thought I'd see a purple waffle plant, either, but every once in a while I stumble across one. Right now I have a waffle plant hanging, appropriately, in my kitchen.

This wide-spreading, vining plant has reddish branches and purple leaves that are pocked with waffle-like depressions.

Contrary to my general rule that brightly colored foliage will do best in bright light, the waffle plant prefers a shady location. It will burn up in a western or southern exposure, and really prefers a northern window. Keep the soil moist, and spray it daily, but *please* don't spray it with syrup!

SPECIFIC CARE REQUIREMENTS

Light: This plant prefers low light.
Water: Keep the soil moist.
Humidity: Medium. Spray this plant daily.
Temperature: Medium. 50 to 70 degrees.

Propagate from stem cuttings.

Rabbit's-foot Fern

DAVALLIA FEJEENSIS

This beautiful, unusual fern gets its nickname from the brown, hairy, footlike roots (known botanically as *rhizomes*) that creep over the sides of the pot. The fronds are light green and delicate and grow on dark brown, wiry stems.

Like all ferns, this plant needs indirect light, lots of water, and lots of spraying. It would love a summer vacation in a shady spot outdoors. Again, you must remember that ferns do not like bright light and dry heat.

SPECIFIC CARE REQUIREMENTS

Light: Medium light. Keep out of direct sunlight.

Water: Keep the soil moist at all times. Do not allow this plant to dry out.

Humidity: High. Spray two or three times a day if possible.

Temperature: Medium. 55 to 75 degrees.

Propagate by dividing the rhizomes in the spring.

Sago Palm

CYCADS REVOLUTA

I particularly like the looks of this palmlike tree. Not only is the foliage extremely striking, but the reddish-brown, rough, slightly hairy trunk can take on some wonderful, bulbous shapes.

I also like this plant because it's practically impossible to kill. Keep it in eastern or filtered western light, and only water it when the soil dries out. (Unlike true palms, the cycads prefer to dry out between waterings.)

Really, this is a wonderful, rewarding plant, which, unlike true palms, won't need any special attention. So, if you see a sago, I say go—for it, that is.

SPECIFIC CARE REQUIREMENTS

Light: Bright, filtered light.
Water: Allow the soil to dry out between waterings.
Humidity: Medium. Spray this plant daily.
Temperature: Medium. 50 to 75 degrees.

Propagate from offsets.

Screw-pine

PANDANUS VEITCHII

This is a really easy-to-care-for plant—if you like its cactusy look. The screw-pine, which has no resemblance or relation to a pine whatsoever, has leaves with sharp, serrated edges and grows in the shape of a spiral rosette. Its deep green color, accented by red spines, makes it an attractive plant, if somewhat stiff.

Keep it in bright, filtered light and let the soil dry out thoroughly between waterings, and it will practically grow by itself.

The only problem you might encounter with this plant will be entire lower leaves—and the tips of others—drying and browning as the plant grows upward. Don't worry; this is natural. Cut the dead leaves off and manicure the tips of the others. Spraying more often may help prevent this problem.

SPECIFIC CARE REQUIREMENTS

Light: Bright, filtered light is best.
Water: Allow the soil to dry out between waterings.
Humidity: Medium. Spray daily.
Temperature: Medium. 50 to 75 degrees.

Propagate from offsets.

Sensitive Plant
or Action Plant

MIMOSA PUDICA

What is the magic appeal of the sensitive, or action, plant? The slightest touch on its dark green, feathery leaves will cause them to close up tightly, to reopen only several minutes later, when it seems to sense that danger has passed. (This reaction may be the plant's defense against herbivores.)

The sensitive plant can be difficult to cultivate outside of a greenhouse, but it is possible. Give the plant filtered eastern light and—this is the key to success— keep the humidity as high as possible.

The sensitive plant is a wonderful curiosity that's especially loved by kids of all ages. These plants are usually small and inexpensive when put up for sale, so always buy one when you run across it.

SPECIFIC CARE REQUIREMENTS

Light: Filtered light.
Water: Keep the soil moist.
Humidity: High. Spray this plant daily and keep it on a pebble tray.
Temperature: Warm. 65 to 85 degrees.

Propagate from seeds.

Shrimp Plant

BELOPERONE GUTTATA

The shrimp plant is a *delicious* hanging plant—or, at least, a real feast for your eyes when it's in bloom.

It has oval, green, somewhat hairy leaves that grow on woody stems. With proper care, the shrimp plant will produce shrimp-colored flowers, hanging from the ends of the stems, almost all year long.

B. guttata needs bright light, moist soil, high humidity, and weekly feedings with flower food during spring and summer.

Normally the shrimp plant won't flower during the winter because it's dormant from late November through early March. But if you start feeding it with a commercial plant food in the second week of March you'll probably be able to coax it into bloom a little earlier than it would on its own.

SPECIFIC CARE REQUIREMENTS

Light: Bright light.

Water: Keep the soil moist.

Humidity: Medium to high. Spray this plant at least once a day, and preferably twice.

Temperature: Medium. 55 to 70 degrees. Keep this plant away from extremely dry heat or extremely cold drafts.

Propagate from stem cuttings.

Snow Rose

SERISSA FOETIDA VARIEGATA

The snow rose is a delightful plant—and one of the most popular for making a small standard or a bonsai. (See the sections on "Bonsai" and "Standards.") This dwarf shrub has tiny, elliptical, dark green leaves with cream-colored margins and a cream-colored midrib.

If kept in a bright western or southern window, watered regularly (to keep the soil slightly moist), misted frequently, and fed once a week during the spring and summer, your *Serissa* will produce a profusion of tiny, white, miniature "roses."

If the leaves start to turn yellow and drop off, feed the plant with Miracle-Gro with "chelate"—an iron supplement.

As a bonsai, the plant can be kept as low as six inches. (A bonsai "forest" is shown here.) As a small standard it usually reaches a height of about two feet. I have a small *Serissa* standard sitting alongside a small dwarf myrtle standard on my living room windowsill, and the pair make a spectacular addition to my plant collection, especially when both are bursting with blooms.

SPECIFIC CARE REQUIREMENTS

Light: Bright or bright, filtered light. A western or southern exposure is best, although the plant will do fine in an eastern window.

Water: Keep the soil moist. This may require daily waterings during the hot summer months.

Humidity: Medium. Spray this plant daily.

Temperature: Medium. 55 to 75 degrees.

Propagate from stem cuttings.

Spanish Moss

TILLANDSIA USNEIODES

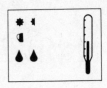

You may have seen this silvery-gray, rootless beauty hanging off the branches of trees in places as diverse and far-ranging as Canada, Florida, or semitropical South America. It hangs in long, stringy clumps that can grow up to twenty-five feet long.

Spanish moss is the ultimate air plant—those ephiphytic wonders that get all the nutrition they need right out of the air instead of the soil. This fascinating and extremely decorative plant is *not* a moss but a bromeliad. It *loves* the shade. Mist it daily and add a teaspoonful of plant food to the misting water once a month.

You can use Spanish moss for indoor decor—hang it from the branches of treelike plants for a very dramatic effect. It's also very pretty growing out of a pot—hiding the soil while at the same time cascading down over the sides.

Since it is used so often as a decorative accent, Spanish moss is usually available (in bags) at any good nursery, plant store, or flower shop.

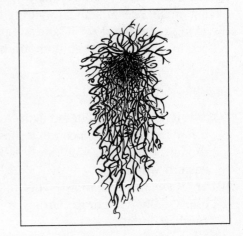

SPECIFIC CARE REQUIREMENTS

Light: A shady location is best, but this plant will tolerate bright, filtered light.
Water: Not necessary because it's not grown in soil.
Humidity: Medium. Spray this plant daily.
Temperature: Medium. 55 to 75 degrees.

Propagate from offsets.

Spider Plant

CHLOROPHYTUM COMOSUM *and*
C. COMOSUM VARIEGATUM

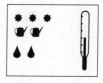

The spider plant is one of the most popular hanging plants, and a real joy to grow if you can get it to produce the spiderlike "babies" that give it its nickname.

The spider plant is a low-growing rosette of green or green-and-white, thin, pointed leaves. Long green or white tendrils emerge from the plant, then produce white, starlike flowers, which turn into baby plantlets with aerial roots.

Hang this plant in a window where it will get bright or bright, filtered sun, and keep the soil slightly moist. Be sure to spray it daily to help keep the leaf tips from turning brown.

Many people complain they can't get their plants to produce babies. My advice, which works, is keep the plant's roots potbound and follow the care instructions below. You'll soon be the proud father or mother (or would that be grandfather or grandmother?) of tons of baby spiders.

To establish new plants, clip about two inches off the end of the stolon, or stem, or umbilical cord, or whatever you want to call it. Plant the spider plantlet in potting soil in a three-inch pot, keep it in bright sun, and keep the soil slightly damp. Transplant it into a larger container when the crown is about six inches across.

An interesting note about the spider plant: A few months ago the government issued a report on the enormously important role that houseplants play in filtering certain poisons from the air. The most useful of these plants were spider plants and philodendrons. How rewarding can you get?

SPECIFIC CARE REQUIREMENTS

Light: Bright or bright, filtered light.
Water: Keep the soil slightly moist.
Humidity: Medium. Spray this plant daily to help avoid brown tips and to feed the roots of the hanging plantlets.
Temperature: Medium. 55 to 75 degrees.

Propagate by planting plantlets.

Staghorn Fern

PLATYCERIUM BIFURCATUM

If you've got the room, a staghorn fern is really a dramatic plant. Hung on a board on a wall, this striking plant (also known as the elk's-horn fern) could be mistaken for a hunter's trophy. Its leathery, gray-green fronds grow up to three feet long, spreading from their base to form two or three wide forks at the tips of the fronds.

The staghorn fern—another epiphytic plant—is easy to raise. Make sure it gets only filtered light. The key to success, though, is frequent misting.

You can propagate new staghorn ferns from the offsets that grow at the base of the plant. These will look like miniature staghorns—because that's what they are. Remove them (carefully!) from the sides of the mother plant with a sharp knife or single-edged razor blade, then plant them in four-inch pots filled with a mixture of half sphagnum moss and half potting mix.

When the plants have developed at least a six-inch wingspan they can be attached to a redwood board or planted in a wire basket filled with sphagnum moss.

SPECIFIC CARE REQUIREMENTS

Light: Filtered light is fine. If you take your staghorn fern outdoors for a summer vacation, be sure to keep it in the shade.
Water: If hung on a board or in a basket, the plant should be dunked in a pail of water once a week.
Humidity: High. Spray this plant a couple of times a day.
Temperature: 55 to 70 degrees. This plant can't tolerate extremely high heat unless the humidity level is equally high.

Propagate from offsets that will grow from the base of the plant.

Strawberry Begonia or Strawberry Geranium

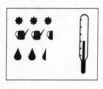

SAXIFRAGA STOLONIFERA

This very interesting and attractive hanging plant has green, roundish, hairy, spotted leaves with purple undersides. It isn't a begonia, a strawberry, or a geranium—but its distinctive foliage and strawberrylike runners make it look a little bit like a combination of all three.

It can be hung in a pot or placed on a shelf, but wherever it is the key to succeeding with this plant is to make sure it gets good, bright sunlight. If you let it dry out between waterings and spray it daily, the strawberry begonia will produce quite pretty little white flowers during the summer. This plant can tolerate fairly shady locations, but the brighter the light the more runners you'll get—and the more likely the plant will be to flower.

For best results add some peat moss or humus to the soil—about three-quarters potting mix to one-quarter humus.

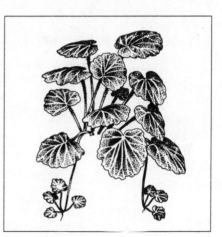

SPECIFIC CARE REQUIREMENTS

Light: Bright or bright, filtered light.
Water: Allow the soil to dry out between waterings.
Humidity: Medium. Spray this plant daily.
Temperature: Medium. 55 to 75 degrees.

Propagate by planting the plantlets that appear at the ends of the stems.

String-of-hearts or Rosary Vine

CEROPEGIA WOODII

This beauty can live up to either of its common nicknames: the string-of-hearts or the rosary vine. Either way, it's a hanging plant with trailing, threadlike leaves marbled with silver. Each pair of leaves is separated by a round, beadlike nodule.

This spectacular specimen is prized by collectors and—because of its unusual appearance—is also a great plant for kids.

Although it is a succulent, string-of-hearts must be kept out of direct sunlight—a filtered eastern exposure is best. And remember to let the soil dry out between waterings. Incidentally, the string-of-hearts prefers sandy soil—so pot it in a soil mixture made of one-half potting soil and one-half sand.

Properly cared for, this plant can live up to twenty years or more. Propagate by hanging a pot of *Ceropegia* next to a pot filled only with soil. Push the ends of some of the stems into the soil of the adjacent pot. They will root and produce a beautiful new plant.

SPECIFIC CARE REQUIREMENTS

Light: Filtered light. Bright, direct sunlight can kill this plant.

Water: Allow the soil to dry out between waterings.

Humidity: Low. Spray this plant once or twice a week.

Temperature: Medium to cool. Between 45 and 70 degrees.

Propagate from stem cuttings.

String-of-pearls

SENECIO ROWLEYANUS

This low-growing plant makes a spectacular hanging succulent. The string-of-pearls is one of my favorites because of its unusual look: It produces stringlike stems upon which grow round, green, pealike balls.

It's not only eye-catching, it is also relatively easy to care for: The keys are bright sunlight and dryish soil. If the "pearls" begin to shrivel up, you're not giving your string-of-pearls enough light.

Of all the thousands of plant nicknames, I think *Senecio rowleyanus* has the most appropriate. And a good thing, too!

SPECIFIC CARE REQUIREMENTS

Light: Bright or bright, filtered light at the very least.

Water: Allow the soil to dry out completely between waterings.

Humidity: Low. Spray this plant once or twice a week.

Temperature: Medium. 55 to 75 degrees.

Propagate from stem cuttings.

Swedish Ivy

PLECTRANTHUS *ssp.*

This creeping herb, often called Creeping Charlie, has small, leathery, bright green, waxy leaves, which are roundish and slightly ruffled at the edges.

It will thrive if you put it in filtered eastern light and keep the soil slightly moist. It's actually a fairly easy plant to grow, but you must pinch back new growth frequently to keep the plant from becoming straggly.

The most famous Swedish ivy in the world sits on a mantlepiece in the White House. Since the days of JFK it's been in the background of every photograph taken of foreign dignitaries visiting the president. It's not the same plant, of course, but according to the head gardener at the White House each new plant has been propagated from one of its predecessors. A real American dynasty!

SPECIFIC CARE REQUIREMENTS

Light: Filtered light.
Water: Keep the soil slightly moist.
Humidity: Spray this plant daily.
Temperature: Medium. 55 to 75 degrees.

Propagate from stem cuttings.

Swiss Cheese Plant

MONSTERA DELICIOSA

Another highly dependable houseplant, this easy-to-care-for climber has long aerial roots and large, thick, leathery leaves—perforated with oblong holes—that give the leaves the appearance of thin slices of green Swiss cheese.

The ideal conditions for this plant are filtered eastern sunlight and a good watering as soon as the soil dries out. Sometimes new leaves will fail to develop holes. If this happens, move the plant into a slightly brighter location and begin feeding it once a week during spring and summer.

The evolution of perforated and split-leaf plants is interesting: Because they climb and are subject to everything from breezes to high winds in their native habitats—usually within tropical forests—they've developed the holes to keep them from blowing off the stems, just as you see flags and hanging signs with holes in them.

Incidentally, under ideal conditions this plant will produce an edible fruit that smells and tastes somewhat like pineapple (hence *deliciosa*), so you can have fruit and cheese for the same price!

SPECIFIC CARE REQUIREMENTS

Light: Medium. Filtered, indirect light is fine.
Water: Allow the soil to dry out between waterings.
Humidity: Medium. Mist this plant daily.
Temperature: Medium. 50 to 75 degrees.

Propagate from stem cuttings.

Table Fern

PTERIS *ssp.*

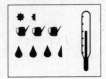

This is another excellent terrarium plant. It's small, about three or four inches tall and two to three inches across. Its leathery, bright green fronds are sometimes variegated with white or cream-colored markings. These graceful fronds grow on dark brown, wirelike stems.

Because this plant loves shade and humidity, the best place to grow it is in a terrarium or bottle garden. If you want to grow it outside of a terrarium, keep it in a northern (shady) exposure, keep the soil moist at all times, and—this is key— spray it at least twice a day and keep it on a dry well. Without *lots* of humidity your *Pteris* will dry up and die.

It also helps to grow this plant in a soil mixture of two-thirds potting mix and one-third peat moss.

SPECIFIC CARE REQUIREMENTS

Light: Low. This plant likes the shade.
Water: Keep the soil moist.
Humidity: High. Spray this plant at least twice a day and keep it on a pebble tray.
Temperature: Medium. 50 to 70 degrees.

Propagate by division.

Urn Plant
or Air Pine

AECHMEA *spp.*

The urn plant is probably the most popular bromeliad. It's certainly the most widely available. You'll see it in flower shops, nurseries, and garden centers all year long.

Also known as the living vase or fascination flower, this plant has large, powdery-looking, grayish-green leaves, but what will catch your eye is the spectacular, spiky, rose-and-blue flower that emerges on a stalk from the center of its "urn."

They're very easy to care for: Just make sure that the plant gets filtered eastern sunlight, and put fresh water in the cup of the plant every day. For best results, grow the urn plant in osmunda fiber instead of potting soil.

I have good news and bad news about this plant's glorious flowering. The bad news is that the urn plant blooms only once during its lifetime (which can last years and years). The good news is that it will also produce profusions of baby plants, or "pups," over the years, and each of these will in turn bloom and produce its own pups.

You can help force an urn plant to bloom by putting half an apple in the center of the plant and then covering the plant with airtight plastic. Ethylene gases from the apple will help stimulate the bloom.

SPECIFIC CARE REQUIREMENTS

Light: Filtered light.
Water: Keep fresh water in the center cup of the plant and allow the soil to dry out between waterings.
Humidity: Medium. Spray this plant daily.
Temperature: Medium. 55 to 75 degrees.

Propagate by removing the pups from the mother plant and planting them.

Venus Flytrap

DIONAEA MUSCIPULA

The Venus flytrap is the legendary queen of the carnivorous plants, as well as the insatiable, saber-toothed central character of *The Little Shop of Horrors*.

In real life, the Venus flytrap can be described as a light green carnivorous perennial. The leaf at the end of each stem is divided into two halves, each with tiny "teeth" that close up when "hairs" on the inside of the leaf are agitated. Insects, lured into the mouth of the plant by color and scent, are clamped into an inescapable trap where enzymes "digest" them and keep the plant thriving. This plant, obviously, is grown as a curiosity instead of for decor.

The best place to grow a Venus flytrap is in a terrarium exposed to filtered light. This will protect the plant from dry, killing air, and you from its snapping jaws! Grow this plant in sphagnum moss instead of soil—it needs the acid soil sphagnum provides—and remember to keep your moss damp!

In captivity, the Venus flytrap will have to be fed from time to time. You can either give it a fly (ugh!) or tiny bits of hamburger. Kids get a great kick out of tickling the inside of a Venus flytrap with a matchstick or somesuch and watching the jaws clamp shut.

P.S. A botanist friend of mind asked me to add this note: Try to make sure that the plant you buy has been grown from seed—not dug up in the wild. Save the wild Venus flytrap!

SPECIFIC CARE REQUIREMENTS

Light: Bright, filtered light is best, although this plant can survive in a shadier location.

Water: High. Keep the potting mixture extremely moist.

Humidity: High. This plant will grow best in a terrarium.

Temperature: Medium. 65 to 85 degrees.

Propagate from seeds.

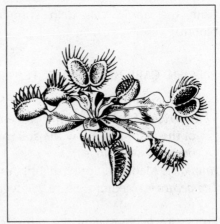

Wandering Jew

ZEBRINA PENDULA

Also known as the flowering inch plant, the wandering Jew comes in many sizes, shapes, and colors. The most common variety has deep green or purple leaves with two broad silver bands—and reddish-purple undersides. Another has small, oval, succulent leaves that are light green or light green and white. A bushy, tiny-leafed, purplish variety—called bridal veil—is considered a variety of wandering Jew but is more correctly *Gibasis geniculata*. There are also varieties that are members of the genus *Tradescantia*.

Care for all of these species and varieties in the same way: Hang the plant in bright, filtered western or southern sunlight, so that it won't lose its color, and keep the soil moist. Spray the plant daily. Be careful not to water directly into the crown of the plant—this will cause an unsightly "bald spot." Pay special attention to the temperature around your plant—too much dry heat during the winter will do this plant in.

If you want to keep your wandering Jew from getting long and straggly, pinch back new growth frequently and cut back about a fourth of the plant at the beginning of winter.

SPECIFIC CARE REQUIREMENTS

Light: Bright, filtered light. Not enough light and the plant will lose its luster.
Water: Keep the soil moist. Be careful not to water into the crown of the plant.
Humidity: Medium. Spray this plant daily.
Temperature: Medium. 55 to 75 degrees. Be careful not to let the plant overheat during the winter.

Propagate from stem cuttings.

Wax Plant
or *Hindu Rope Plant*

HOYA CARNOSA

Also called the porcelain flower, this succulent vining plant has waxy, oval, light green leaves, usually splashed with white, but sometimes a plain light green. The variety commonly called Hindu rope is probably the more interesting of the two. Its vines grow like a tight, long curl—sometimes trailing as long as four or five feet down from the plant. Both varieties will produce clusters of dainty pinkish flowers if properly tended.

Remember, this is a succulent. As a general rule of green thumb, all cacti and succulents need good, bright light, especially if you want them to flower. Add water only when the soil is dry. The leaves will start to crinkle up if your wax plant isn't getting enough water.

SPECIFIC CARE REQUIREMENTS

Light: Bright light.

Water: Allow the soil to dry out completely between waterings.

Humidity: Low. Spray this plant once a week, but more often when it's in bloom.

Temperature: Medium. 55 to 75 degrees.

Propagate from stem cuttings.

Weeping Fig

FICUS BENJAMINA

Easily the most popular of all the indoor trees, the weeping fig owes its appeal, I'd bet, to the fact that it looks so much like an outdoor tree. It has shiny little dark green leaves that spring from woody branches and a woody stem. The droopy look is very attractive. There is also a variegated variety whose leaves have cream-colored edges.

The one big problem with weeping figs: They almost always drop their leaves at least once a year. I've had trees that have gone completely bare. People who aren't familiar with this habit will think their weeping fig is dying. Take Mr. Mother Earth's word for it—it's not. This is a completely natural process. The leaves will grow back in a couple of months, just the way this plant's deciduous brother and sister trees act outdoors.

Keep your weeping fig in the brightest spot you've got, and keep the soil moist during this period—and new leaf buds should soon appear.

SPECIFIC CARE REQUIREMENTS

Light: Bright or bright, filtered light. This tree will fail in inadequate light.
Water: Allow the soil to dry out between waterings.
Humidity: Medium. Spray this plant daily.
Temperature: Medium. Between 50 and 75 degrees.

Propagate from stem cuttings.

Yucca

YUCCA ALOIFOLIA

I think the yucca is a most rewarding houseplant because it is durable and because it makes a great decorative desertlike statement in a southern or western corner—giving your room an authentic southwestern desertlike look.

Some people don't like the stiff, almost menacing look of the yucca plant, with its long, pale green, sharp-pointed leaves growing in the shape of a tree from the sides of a thick, woody stem. You'll have to decide for yourself.

If you do choose to add a yucca to your collection, make sure that you provide a bright, sunny location, and be sure to water it only when the soil dries out. The plant doesn't need much humidity, and as it grows taller the lower leaves will dry up and fall off. This is natural, and there really isn't anything you can do to prevent it. In the wild, a sixty-foot-tall yucca plant looks great with only the top thirty feet bearing foliage. In your home, though, half a yucca is better than none, but probably not as good as one.

If your plant gets too bare, saw off the top third of the plant, including the foliage, and put it in a container of water. New roots will form within a month or so, and then you can pot up the new plant and start all over again. The remaining old stalk, kept in bright sunlight and watered when dry, will sprout new growth from its sides.

SPECIFIC CARE REQUIREMENTS

Light: Bright light.
Water: Low. Water only when dry.
Humidity: Minimal.
Temperature: Medium. 55 to 80 degrees.

Propagate from cuttings.

PART THREE

Many More Rewards

SPECIALTIES OF
THE HOUSE

I know that many of you will want to expand your plant experiences beyond cultivating these beautiful plants. Although personally I find growing the plants rewarding enough, I always keep fresh herbs on my kitchen windowsill; I've had lots of fun growing plants from the pits and seeds in my grocery bag; I love standards and topiaries, and think they make wonderful decorative accents and stunning gifts; and although I've never gotten into making my own bonsai plants, I find them among my favorite works of art. So here, for the more adventurous among you, are a few ideas that will make your indoor gardening even more rewarding.

GROW YOUR
OWN HERBS

Growing herb plants can be one of the greatest joys of indoor gardening. Not only are they beautiful to look at and fun to grow, but as both an indoor gardener and a vegetarian cook, I can assure you there's nothing more rewarding than seasoning your favorite dish with a bit of oregano, thyme, or sage that you grew yourself.

I'm often asked about the difference between herbs and spices. Well, botanists generally refer to herbs—derived from the Latin *herba*, meaning grass—as "herbaceous plants whose stems are soft and succulent rather than woody."

For most of the rest of us, herbs are any of a large number of plants, both herbaceous *and* woody, that grow in relatively temperate climates and whose leaves and stems can be used for culinary purposes or for giving off delightful fragrances, have proven curative powers, or can be used as natural cosmetics or dyes. Herbs can also be dried to make beautiful wreathes or breathtaking potpourris.

A spice, on the other hand, is generally a very aromatic or strongly flavored substance—obtained from the seeds, roots, flowers, or bark of a plant—that can be used in the same way.

Sometimes plants can be both herbs and spices: The coriander plant is an herb, generally known as cilantro or Chinese parsley, while ground coriander seeds are classified as a spice.

Almost all herbs are scented, but the most fragrant herbs are bay, lavender, scented geraniums, lemon verbena, patchouli, and tansy. Herbs used for dyeing and coloring include indigo (for blue), agrimony (for yellow), and madder root (for red). And people have been using herbs—such as chamomile for tea and aloe vera, applied topically, for rashes and burns—for medicinal purposes since the beginning of time.

The culinary herbs (used for flavoring foods) include anise, basil, bay, chervil, chives, dill, fennel, mint, mustard, oregano, parsley, rosemary, sage, savory, thyme, and many more. They can be used either fresh or dried. Just remember that dried herbs are stronger than fresh herbs—one tablespoon of fresh herbs equals one teaspoon of dry herbs. Also, you should add fresh herbs relatively late in the cooking process so that you don't cook out all the subtle, delicate flavor.

There are a number of different ways to dry herbs. You can hang harvested bunches of fresh herbs in a dark, well-ventilated place for up to fourteen days, at which time they'll be dry and crumbly; you can put them on a tray set on a sunny windowsill—where they'll dry in about a week; you can dry them on a tray in a 400-degree oven for five or ten minutes; or, if you're really in a hurry, you can pop a couple of cupfuls of herb leaves into a microwave oven for about three minutes.

The good news is that almost every herb, ranging from tender annuals (which complete their growth cycle and return to seed in one season) to hardy perennials (which survive year after year, even when the temperature drops well below freezing), will grow outdoors in the United States. The better news is that many herbs will flourish indoors, in containers, all year long.

HOW TO GET GROWING

The most rewarding route toward growing your own herbs is to start them from seeds. You'll find a large variety of packeted herb seeds in nurseries, garden centers, and discount stores, beginning in late winter. You should begin planting in early spring.

Follow the directions on the seed packet, which will read something like this: Fill a pan or a low, wide pot with one-half commercial potting mix, one-quarter vermiculite, and one-quarter perlite. Plant the seeds in rows about four inches apart and about half an inch under the soil. Keep the soil moist and in a bright, warm spot.

The seeds should sprout within two weeks. As the individual plantlets reach heights of three to four inches, weed out the smallest, scrawniest seedlings, and plant the strongest into individual small pots about two inches in diameter. Keep them in bright sunlight and keep the soil moist (this usually requires daily watering). Within a few weeks you should have flourishing plantlets that are anywhere from six inches to a foot tall and ready to be transplanted into and cultivated in four-inch pots.

As fresh herbs become more and more popular in cooking, people are also buying established herb plants, usually in four-inch pots. You can find high-quality plants in better nurseries and garden centers almost all year long. (And a great mail order catalog is available from Well-Sweep Herb Farm, 317 Mt. Bethel Road, Port Murray, NJ 07865.)

Although you can buy perennial herb plants during the fall and winter, the best time to buy is during early spring or summer, so that they can get a good roothold in your house or apartment. When buying herb plants, make sure they're healthy: A good plant is full, bushy, and free of drying leaves. When you get your plants home, just pop them onto a sunny windowsill and water them often so that the soil does not dry out.

The general rules for keeping herbs thriving indoors, even during the winter months, are:

Light: Herb plants need at least five hours of good sunlight every day during the hot summer months. If you cannot provide enough natural sunlight, herbs will do very well under artificial lights.

Water: Keep the soil slightly moist at all times.

Humidity: Most herb plants like medium to high humidity; otherwise their tiny foliage will dry out. Spray them daily and, for maximum results, keep them on a dry well.

Soil: A regular commercial potting mix is fine, but I suggest you add a bit of perlite to create a lighter soil and ensure good drainage.

Food: Herb plants need very little food, but you should feed them once a month from early spring through late summer.

Harvesting Your Herbs: Whether you're growing your herbs for cooking, for fragrance, or for medicinal use, you'll want to harvest them frequently. I'd suggest cutting a couple of inches off the tops every time your herb plants grow that much. This will not only keep you well-supplied with herbs but will help encourage bushy new growth as well. You can harvest herbs using scissors, or by just pinching off the less woody tops, any time you like.

THESE ARE A FEW OF MY FAVORITE HERBS

These five herbs—oregano, thyme, savory, sage, and rosemary—are my favorites because they are all hardy perennials that will grow in your home year-round. In short, these are the most dependable and most rewarding herbs. Here are my recommendations for each:

Oregano: Oregano is almost interchangeable with another delicious perennial, sweet marjoram, but has a slightly sharper flavor. It makes a *wonderful* container plant, growing into a shrub about two feet tall with dark green, oval leaves.

Oregano should be grown in full sunlight, but make sure to keep the soil moist. It can be propagated from seeds, cuttings, or root division.

Oregano is an especially good addition to dishes such as pasta, soups, salad, and tomato-based recipes. The dish I think of first when I think of oregano is minestrone. Dee-licious!

Thyme: There are hundreds of species of this very pungent and useful herb—which is pronounced "time." The three varieties that are most popular among indoor gardeners are the Doone Valley variety, the colorful silver thyme *(Thymus vulgaris variegata)*, and German winter thyme. I recommend the Doone Valley variety. It's a perennial evergreen, at most twelve inches high, with narrow, dark green or gray-green aromatic leaves and purplish-pink flowers.

This woody perennial will thrive in full sun, if kept slightly moist, and in light, well-drained soil. You should clip (or harvest) your thyme plant frequently or it will develop woody stems. Propagate new plants from seeds or stem cuttings.

Thyme can be used effectively with meats, poultry, stews, sauces, and soups. I make a mean zucchini loaf flavored with thyme.

Savory: There are several varieties of savory, but the two most common are winter savory *(Satureja montana)* and summer savory *(S. hortensis)*. Winter savory is a hardy perennial that will grow almost two feet tall. It can withstand relatively severe winter temperatures if grown outdoors, and will do very well on your kitchen windowsill. Summer savory is an annual that has a slightly more delicate flavor, but I don't recommend that you try to grow it indoors. Both varieties have small, needlelike leaves and produce tiny, pinkish-white flowers.

All savories, like most herb plants, require full sun and constant moisture. The winter savory prefers soil with more sand in it than does its summer brother— and is propagated by division or root cuttings.

Savory is delicious in soups, stews, and my recipe for three-bean salad.

Sage: Another hardy perennial, sage is a member of the mint family *(Salvia)*. Besides its culinary value, sage has long been used as a medicinal herb—for everything from upset stomachs to baldness. In medieval times sage was even thought to improve the memory.

I can't vouch for its medicinal value, but sage does add a great flavor to many dishes. The most common indoor variety is *Salvia vulgaris*, which can grow to a height of over two feet. It has gray-green, oval leaves, and violet-colored flowers appear on tall spikes in early summer. Another wonderful variety of sage is *S. elegans*, or pineapple sage, whose light green leaves have a strong pineapple aroma. Other varieties include *S. guaranticia*, *S. officianalus*, and the showy variegated variety, *S.* "Tricolor".

Sage, like most herbs, needs full sun, well-drained soil, and can be propagated by seeds or stem cuttings.

It is delicious fresh or dried, and goes well with sausage, pork chops, vegetables, or pasta sauce. The most traditional use for sage is at Thanksgiving, in turkey stuffing.

Rosemary: Rosemary *(Rosmarinas off.* "Prostatus") is more woody than the average herb plant, and you'll often see it as a small standard or as even a bonsai plant. The leaves are usually green, gray-green, or blue-green needles, and the blooms grow in clusters of lavender or blue.

Although rosemary needs full sun, you should only water it when the soil is dry. Rosemary grows up to six feet tall and should be kept away from cold drafts during the winter months. Propagate this plant from cuttings or by division—the seeds are tricky to germinate.

Rosemary is said to alleviate headaches, heal wounds, and induce sleep, but it's most prized as a flavorful addition to meats, soups, and vegetables. And for a summer treat I sprinkle fresh rosemary leaves on my homemade fruit salad.

Using fresh herbs as flavoring can often turn a very good dish into a gourmet's delight. But, even if you choose to dry some of the herbs you grow and harvest, you'll get a great deal more satisfaction from sprinkling home-grown rosemary into a recipe than from adding the same herb from a store-bought jar.

It's time for you to join the ever-growing ranks of those who have discovered the pleasures of cultivating their own herbs. Whether you decide to start your herbs from seeds, cuttings, or if you buy established plants, good luck, happy growing, and bon appetit!

PLANTS FROM PITS

Like most people, I was introduced to "grocery bag gardening" as a child. I was amazed that you could put an avocado pit into a glass of water or a pot of soil and, as if by magic, a beautiful plant would eventually appear.

It wasn't until years later that I discovered—at a flower show in New York—that you can also grow such exotic subtropical plants as mangos, papayas, litchis, macadamias, starfruit, coconuts, pecans, and tamarinds from the pits of fruit you've bought at a supermarket or green grocer. You can also grow citrus, kiwis, guavas, loquats, passion fruit, persimmons, and pineapples—all in pots in your house or apartment.

Of course, as Mr. Mother Earth I knew that if you lived in a warm, tropical climate such as California, Florida, or Hawaii, you'd be surrounded by these magnificent trees, bent with fruit in their seasons, sprouting around you on practically an hour-to-hour basis.

But actually to grow them on a windowsill? It seems too good to be true. But it isn't, and I've got "plants-from-pits" thriving on my kitchen windowsill to prove it. Unfortunately, most of these plants won't produce edible fruit grown indoors, but so what? Their beautiful, lush, unusual foliage is rewarding enough.

Although the basic planting and care instructions are the same—easy—for most of these plants, here are some hints that will give you a much better chance of succeeding with them.

First, of course, you must obtain the fruit with the pits. Most of the fruit is available from supermarkets or green grocers, but some of the more exotic ones, such as the starfruit (carambolas), tamarind, fresh litchi nuts, or macadamias might be difficult to locate. (*Seeds* for these plants, along with rhizomes for bananas and fig tree cuttings, can be obtained from the sources listed at the end of this chapter.)

Once you've enjoyed the fruit, remove the pits and plant them in a mix of three-quarters commercial potting soil and one-quarter perlite or vermiculite.

There is no absolute formula as to how deep to plant the pits—in nature the seeds just drop off the trees and sprout where they land. Try planting your seeds about an inch below the top of the soil.

Always plant several seeds, because some will germinate and others will not.

Unfortunately, there's no way to tell which seeds are viable (able to germinate) by just looking at them. (This applies to both store-bought seeds and fresh seeds.) For best results, plant the seeds as soon as you can. The fresher, the better—within two or three days is best.

Keep the pots in bright light and keep the soil warm and moist. In most cases your seeds will sprout within three to four weeks. If they don't germinate and start producing sprouts within a month, give up on them and plant some new ones.

Once the seedlings sprout and reach a height of two or three inches, weed out the weaker plantlets—they'll be obviously smaller and scrawnier than the rest. Repot the stronger, lusher, healthier seedlings into individual two-inch or three-inch pots—in regular commercial potting mix. Once you've repotted your seedlings, start the general care as follows.

GENERAL CARE

The general care for all of these plants is the same: Basically, you're trying to re-create the plants' natural tropical or semitropical atmosphere.

They all need lots of good, bright *light*. If they don't get it, they'll probably fail. A western or southern windowsill or corner is best for almost all of these plants. But wait until the plant is well established—at least six inches high—before putting it into direct light. Until then, be sure it gets bright, but filtered, light.

Water often enough that the soil doesn't dry out. Test the soil with your finger regularly. As soon as the top half-inch or so is dry to the touch, water the plant thoroughly—so that the excess runs out of the bottom of the pot. You may have to water every day during the summer and only a couple of times a week during the winter, but make sure the soil is always moist.

As you would expect from plants whose natural habitats are tropical isles (or at least warm, humid places), plants-from-pits need lots of *humidity*. Spray them daily and keep them on dry wells. Don't forget to check the dry well every day to be sure the water is close to the top of the pebbles. If possible, group all of your plants together—with a humidifier running nearby. Your collection will be a great conversation piece and the humidity will be ideal.

All of these plants prefer *temperatures* on the warm side, as long as they're getting enough humidity. Too much warmth and not enough humidity will cause the plant to dry up and die. Don't let the temperature drop below 55 degrees—and remember that cold winter drafts can be deadly.

MY FAVORITE PLANTS-FROM-PITS

Now I'd like to introduce you to some of the plants-from-pits in my own "plant-tation," and give you special tips on how to grow them.

Avocado: Most of us enjoy growing a plant from the pit of an avocado because avocados are readily available all year-round and are very easy to germinate.

The avocado plant is a tall and quite handsome tree, with darkish-green, oval, pointed leaves. New growth is coppery red, and appears throughout the year. Avocado trees will also bear clusters of yellow-white flowers.

Depending on the variety, the avocado fruit can be round or pear-shaped, dark green or light green, leathery-skinned or smooth. The avocado whose pit is used most often for sprouting is *Persea americana*, often called the alligator pear. This is the dark green, almost black, rough-skinned variety.

The pit of the avocado, which is pointed on one end and flat on the other, nestles in a cavity in the center of the fruit.

Begin the germination process by planting your avocado pit directly into a six-inch pot of commercial potting mix, pointy side up, leaving the top one-fourth of the pit above the soil. Make sure you keep the soil moist.

Or—and this is the way we did it when we were kids—you can stand your avocado pit, supported by toothpicks, in a tall glass of water (again, pointy-side-up), submerging the bottom three-quarters of the pit and leaving the top one-quarter above water. *(Ill. 14)*

In either case, with luck, the pit will split, producing a stem and leaves, which will begin to grow upward (although only one out of three avocado pits will succeed). If you've germinated the seed in water, wait until the stem is about four inches long, and then pot it in potting mix, as above.

Keep the plant in a bright, sunny window and keep the soil moist. Spray the plant frequently, because avocado leaves tend to turn brown if they don't get enough humidity. Feed it with commercial houseplant food during the spring and summer. After the stem reaches a height of about one foot, begin pinching off the top growth to encourage bushiness. Your avocado will eventually reach heights of five or six feet.

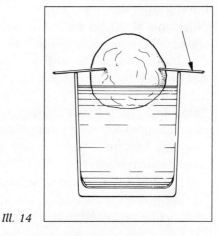

Ill. 14

Citrus (see also Dwarf lemon, page 67, in the chapter on the most rewarding plants): Most members of the citrus family will yield viable pits.

The pits of the various species and hybrids of oranges, lemons, limes, and grapefruits will produce beautiful, woody-stemmed plants with shiny green foliage—that might even flower and fruit within two or three years.

Plant citrus seeds in damp vermiculite or regular potting mix. When plantlets appear, transplant the strongest into four-inch pots with commercial potting mix and cultivate as below. Citrus seeds often take up to six weeks to germinate, so be patient.

The key to succeeding with citrus is adequate light. Keep your citrus plants in bright sunlight—indoors during the winter months and outdoors during spring and summer, if possible. No matter what kind of citrus you plant, it must have at least a western or southern exposure to succeed. Keep the soil moist and the humidity high. Spray the plants daily and keep them on a dry well. And feed them every week during the spring and summer.

Mango (known botanically as *Mangifera indica*): The mango is known as the apple of the tropics—thanks to its year-round abundance and availability. You can now find them year-round in most good American supermarkets as well.

Mango trees have long, narrow, deep green, shiny leaves, and new growth is tinged with red. They also produce very lovely red flowers.

The fruits can be round, oblong, or kidney-shaped. They vary in size from a few ounces to a couple of pounds. The skin can be green, yellow, red, or purple, but usually it's a beautiful blend of all those shades. The fruit itself is yellow-orange, full of fiber, and has the texture of a peach when ripe.

The secret to planting mango pits and being rewarded with a beautiful plant is to remove the pit from inside the fruit, and let it dry out for three or four days. Then push it down flat onto the top of the potting mixture. A root will grow into the soil from the "eye" end of the mango pit and a seedling will emerge from the other end. Don't be surprised if only about one out of two or three mango pits sprout. About as many will rot as will succeed.

Once rooted, place your mango plant in good, bright light, keep the soil damp, and pinch it back frequently to encourage wide and attractive growth.

Tamarind (*Tamarindus indica*): Generally found in Mexican specialty markets, tamarind pods look like plump, brown lima beans and are the fruit of the tamarind tree. The tree itself has feathery leaves and looks almost exactly like a mimosa (see Sensitive plant, page 127). The fleshy, sweet-tart fruit is used to make tea, to add spice to any number of Indian dishes, and is chewed and eaten as is.

The pits are quite easy to grow. Nick them and soak them in water for a couple of hours before planting them in either damp vermiculite or potting mix. Keep the seeds in a bright, sunny, warm spot until they germinate, or sprout. When the seedlings reach a few inches in height, repot the stronger ones into four-inch pots and discard the others.

Keep the plants in good, bright sunlight—a western or southern windowsill is ideal. Give your tamarind lots of humidity, spray it daily, and keep it on a pebble tray. The key to success with this plant, besides giving it enough light, is warmth. The tamarind is very sensitive to cold drafts, so never let the temperature dip below 55 degrees, and be especially watchful of cold drafts in the winter.

Pineapple (see Pineapple, page 118): Pineapples are not grown from pits or seeds, but from the tops of mature pineapples.

Twist, do not cut, the top off a ripe pineapple—choosing one with especially full, bright green, healthy foliage, free of brown tips. Remove the lower leaves until you have a stump about one and a half inches long. You'll find tiny roots on the stump where you've removed the leaves. Allow the top to dry out for a day or two, then plant it in potting mix deep enough so that the stump is submerged below the soil. *(Ill. 15)*

Because the plant is a bromeliad, keep it in bright, filtered light—a western or eastern exposure is fine. Water into the cup of the plant itself, letting the soil dry out completely between waterings. Keep the humidity as high as possible by setting the plant on a pebble tray and spraying it daily. This is the key to success with this plant—not enough humidity and your pineapple will turn brown and shrivel up.

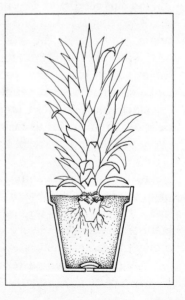

Ill. 15

Coffee *(Coffea arabica)*: A small coffee tree—with bright, shiny, oval-shaped green leaves growing on thin, woody stems—makes a beautiful windowsill plant. The coffee plant is also easy and fun to grow, but there is one important rule to remember: You must plant *unroasted* or green (raw) coffee beans, which are usually available at gourmet coffee shops. You *cannot* plant a roasted bean and expect it to germinate.

Plant the unroasted beans in four-inch pots filled with commercial potting mix. Plant three beans in each pot. If all three plantlets sprout, weed out the two weaker seedlings.

Once you've got your coffee plant started, keep it in a bright spot—a western or southern windowsill. Water it frequently, feeling the soil often and making sure it doesn't dry out completely. Keep the humidity high—spray the plant every day, and keep it on a dry well. Keep the temperature between 55 and 75 degrees, and after three or four years your coffee plant might just develop some bright red beans—maybe even enough to roast.

Litchi: Natives of southern China, litchis (or lychees), are most often seen being served as dessert in Chinese restaurants as a small, pinkish-white fruit floating in a sweet juice.

The litchi plant has soft, green, pinnate leaves about four to six inches long. New growth is a lovely, contrasting coppery pink.

In its natural state the litchi nut is red, slightly nobby, and has a hard shell. The soft, pinkish-white, and deliciously juicy litchi fruit is inside this shell, which peels off rather easily. Inside the fruit is the seed you want to plant.

Put this seed, with its outer skin (or pericarp) intact, directly into a mix of two-thirds potting soil and one-third perlite. Keep this mixture damp and place it in a bright, sunny spot. The seeds should germinate within two weeks.

Litchis are tropical plants, and the key to success with them is high humidity. Bright sun is important, and the plant should be kept moist, but daily spraying and a constantly filled pebble tray are critical.

Once you find fresh litchi nuts you'll be hooked, both by the plants and the delicious fruit. As far as taste is concerned, I must confess that canned litchis are every bit as good as fresh. Except that you won't be able to grow the pits!

Dates *(Phoenix roebeleni)*: Date pits will produce a lovely palm tree. Like most palm seeds, they're slow to germinate. It may take two months before you see the first signs of green emerging from the soil. But it's worth the wait for the beautiful plant that emerges: a very graceful tree with a single, rough trunk topped by a crown of feathery leaves.

Buy packaged, unpasteurized dates, usually found in health stores, and enjoy the sweet, delicious fruit. Then plant the pits, one to a four-inch pot filled with commercial potting mix. Set the pots in good, bright light and then be patient.

Once the plant emerges, keep it in filtered eastern light, keep the soil moist, spray the plant frequently, and in about five years you'll have a beautiful, mature tree.

Macadamia *(Macadamia integrifolia)*: When we think of macadamia nuts we think of Hawaii—and huge trees, thirty to forty feet tall. But you can grow a macadamia tree right on your own sunny windowsill. Indoors, the macadamia tree can grow up to six feet tall.

First, of course, you have to obtain a raw macadamia nut—not the expensive, canned macadamias that have been roasted. The raw macadamia nut develops from the clusters of creamy white flowers that grow on the macadamia tree, which has shiny, leathery, deep green leaves that are from six to ten inches long. The nut itself is a smooth, very hard seed enclosed in a green husk that splits open as the nut matures.

Plant the seeds in four-inch pots. Once the seeds have sprouted—in about three to four weeks—keep them in a filtered western or eastern exposure.

As the plant grows stronger and reaches heights of over a foot, you can move it into a brighter exposure. Macadamias *can* tolerate slightly less light than most of the plants described in this section. Water enough to keep the soil damp, and keep the humidity high by spraying and setting the plant on a pebble tray. Keep the temperature between 55 and 75 degrees. Outdoors, macadamias can tolerate low temperatures, but indoors, avoid cold drafts.

Macadamia seeds are among the easiest to grow, but don't expect nuts—or you'll go nuts! Even outdoors, under optimum tropical conditions, these plants can take as long as twelve years to bear fruit.

Coconuts: No, you won't get to harvest a "lovely bunch of coconuts," but if you get an unhusked coconut, place the whole coconut on top of sandy, damp soil in a large, fourteen-inch-diameter bucket or pot, and keep it warm and in good light, a coconut palm tree will emerge from the end of the "pit." *(Ill. 16)*

Once your coconut sprouts, move it to a spot where it gets bright western or southern sunlight, keep the soil moist, spray it daily, and keep the temperature between 55 and 75 degrees. To grow a coconut palm tree three feet tall indoors might take three years, but the dramatic result is well worth the wait.

Caring for plants-from-pits is roughly equivalent to caring for flowering plants. They need a bit more attention and TLC, but you'll find the fact that you grew them yourself tremendously rewarding. If you have a few failures—if pits rot, or

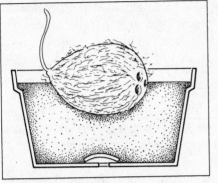

Ill. 16

fail to germinate, or seedlings wilt and die—have faith. It's only a matter of time until the fruits of your labor and patience will be rewarded—maybe even with fruit!

No matter where you live, these subtropical plants can make your living room or sun porch feel like Hawaii or Tahiti. Trust me. When your seeds sprout and you watch them grow into beautiful, bushy, healthy trees, the achievement will be sweeter than the fruit from whence it sprang.

So, get growing to your nearest grocery store or fruit stand, and adopt the motto of seed-and-pit fanciers all over America: "Hug-a-Pit!"

SOURCES:

Exotica Seed Catalog and
Rare Fruit Nursery
2508-B E. Vista Way
Vista, California 92083
619-724-9093

Rare Pit and Plant Council
c/o Sal Scutaro
30 East 10th Street
New York, New York 10003

STANDARDS

To lovers of popular music, a "standard" is a song that will live forever: "Stardust," "Embraceable You," and anything by Irving Berlin or Cole Porter. To teachers or moralists, a "standard" is something set up as a rule or a measure to be followed. To botany buffs, though, a "standard" is a plant that has been painstakingly trained into a tall, slim, bare-trunked tree with a rounded, bushy, flowering-in-season top.

Any plant that tends to grow upright—primarily those with thick or woody stems, such as azalea, hibiscus, *Ficus benjamina*, geranium, or fuchsia—can be trained into a standard. I recommend these plants because they'll make beautiful standards—and survive the winter (indoors) in virtually any climate.

SETTING YOUR OWN STANDARD

To create your own standard, purchase any one of these plants in late March or early April, when they're beginning to grow.

For example, let's say that you want to create a beautiful geranium standard. First, you should buy a single-stem geranium plant that's between six inches and one foot tall. Take it out of its pot and clip off the lower branches and leaves—but leave the top quarter of the plant intact. Now repot the plant in a six-inch pot filled with commercial potting mix.

Take a "green stick," or plant stake (available at any plant store), and push it into the soil right next to the stem of your geranium. The stake should be approximately as tall as you'd like your geranium standard to grow. Make sure that the stake is straight and firmly planted. It will probably support your geranium standard for the lifetime of the plant—which, for a geranium, can be years and years. Now, take some plant ties and bind the stem of the plant to the stake. *(Ill. 17)*

For the first month or two, keep the plant indoors in a bright, warm, well-ventilated spot. Water it often enough to keep the soil slightly moist to the touch, and feed it once a week with a good commercial houseplant fertilizer. *As the plant grows upward, clip or rub off any new growth that appears on the sides of the stem.*

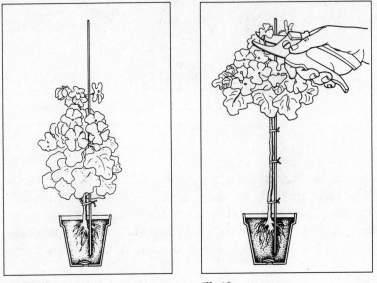

Ill. 17   Ill. 18

Now, if the weather outside has turned consistently mild, move the plant out-doors, making sure that it gets at least four hours of good sunlight every day—since geraniums need lots of good, bright sun to thrive. Water your geranium daily during this period, and continue to feed it once a week with a commercial house-plant food.

As the plant grows, continue to clip off any side growth that appears. This helps keep the trunk slim, smooth, and straight. *(Ill. 18)*

At the end of the summer bring the plant back indoors. Nurture it through the winter by keeping it in your brightest window, spraying it daily, and letting the soil dry out between waterings.

Come the following spring, move your plant outside again. By this time, you'll probably have decided just how tall you want your geranium standard to get. Once it reaches the desired height—and it might very well have grown to as much as three feet tall by the middle of the second summer—*"top" the plant by clipping off the terminal—or top—bud.*

This forces the plant to send out side branches at the top—and begin forming the standard's characteristic "bushy-headed" shape. Keep on watering the plant daily and feeding it weekly, and continue to clip or pinch off new growth at the very top. By the end of the second summer the plant will have developed a lush, thick "head" on top of its straight, slick, sturdy stem.

You can use the same procedure with any plant you might want to shape into a standard. Just make sure to adjust your care to fit the needs of the specific plant.

Does this seem like a lot of trouble to go to to create a plant you could buy?

Not really, when you consider that the same plant purchased at a nursery or garden center would cost you anywhere from $50 to over $400—and you'd lose out on the rewards of doing it yourself.

It will take a couple of years for your home-grown standards to look like the ones in the plant store, but it's fun to try and well worth the wait. A standard plant, like a standard song, can be a thing of beauty and joy, well, if not forever, then at least for a long, long time.

TOPIARY

What is topiary? Some people associate topiary with plants I call "small standards"—plants under three feet tall that have been trained and shaped by pruning into a nearly perfectly rounded ball of foliage on top of a thin, straight, narrow stem. Plants like *Serissa* and rosemary, for example, are used to make these small standards, or topiaries.

To most people, though, topiary is the art of shaping plants into figures of animals or geometric forms.

The oldest known method of forming a topiary is to grow a hedgelike outdoor plant, such as boxwood, and then, over a period of several years, prune it and cut it and eventually create the shape of an elephant, or a horse, or whatever.

But, since we're interested in the rewards of houseplants, let's look at two methods that you can use to make your own ivy-covered heart, dancing bear, graceful swan, cuddly poodle—or a cone or triangle covered with creeping fig—for a showy display on a windowsill or tabletop.

MY TOP TOPIARY TECHNIQUE

For the first method you'll need a hollow, three-dimensional wire frame fashioned in the shape of the topiary you're trying to grow.

You can either buy this frame or try to make it yourself. Many nurseries, flower shops, or garden centers carry topiary frames, or you can order them by mail from Topiary, Inc. (41 Bering, Tampa, Florida 33606). If you're artistic and clever you may want to make the frame yourself, using chicken wire or #10 galvanized wire, some solder, and a soldering iron. You will have to bend and shape the wire into the desired shape, and all I can do is wish you good luck, because I, personally, am not very creative in this area.

Let's say, for example, that you want to create a topiary dog covered with creeping fig. When you begin, your frame should look like a dog made out of wire.

Now take some sphagnum moss, wet it thoroughly in a bucket, and stuff the frame with the damp moss. Pack the moss into the frame tightly. Wrap the moss-filled frame with fishing line to keep the moss inside.

Ill. 19

Next, get several small creeping fig plants to use to cover the moss. I recommend creeping fig because it's easy to grow and will cover the frame very quickly. Make holes for each plant in the damp moss with your finger or a pencil—these holes should be at least an inch deep.

Take individual, rooted strands of creeping fig and tuck them through the wires of the frame into these holes. Pin each piece of creeping fig into place with pieces of wire shaped into clips similar to hairpins.

You can, if you wish, cover the moss-filled shape completely, using as many rooted pieces of creeping fig as it takes. Or you can cover it sparsely and let nature take its course. In other words, you can wait a few weeks, or even months, for the fig to creep naturally over the entire doggy shape. *(Ill. 19)*

In either case, you should keep your fig-covered Fido in filtered light—an eastern exposure is perfect (although this particular plant will tolerate even shadier conditions). Spray it every day to keep the moss moist and the plant growing properly, and give it a complete dunking in a large sink (or bathtub) full of water every other week.

During the spring and summer, feed the foliage of your topiary by mixing your commercial plant food (not kibble!) into your misting water—and spraying the mixture on the topiary. This is called foliar feeding—the plant takes the food in through its breathing cells, or stomata, on the leaves.

TOPIARY FOR BEGINNERS?

A slightly less complex, but equally rewarding way to make a topiary is to bend a piece of wire, or even a coat hanger, into a relatively simple shape such as a circle or a heart; then cover it with a climbing plant such as wax plant or grape ivy.

Start out by purchasing a six-inch pot of grape ivy. I recommend using grape ivy *(Cissus rhombifolia)* instead of English ivy *(Hedera helix)* because *Cissus* is much easier to grow indoors.

For our example, let's say you've decided to create a simple heart-shape.

First, bend a coat hanger or other piece of wire into the desired shape. Your wire circle should look like the round wire antennas on portable TV sets. Leave about two or three inches of wire unbent at each end. Stick these straight ends into the pot of ivy, and then, strand by strand, wrap the ivy around the frame. Wrap some green thread or invisible fishing line around the ivy to hold it in place. Make sure you trim and prune the plant regularly to keep it from growing off wildly from its frame. *(Ill. 20)*

CARING FOR YOUR TOPIARY

How you care for this kind of topiary depends on which plant you use. In almost every case—whether you use grape ivy, creeping fig, wax plant, hoya, or any other small-leafed, low-growing, vining plant—you must spray your topiary every day to keep it from drying out.

Keep the grape ivy topiary in an eastern window, let the soil dry out between waterings, and feed it every other week during the spring and summer.

If you have the creative talent and the patience, you can have lots of fun making your own topiaries, and I assure you that your friends will absolutely love them as gifts.

Ill. 20

BONSAI

Although bonsai is an ancient Japanese art, you don't have to be either ancient or Japanese to do it.

Actually, the literal translation of "bonsai" is "plant in a shallow tray." So though most of us associate bonsai with dwarfing and shaping plants into incredible living sculpture, it really means simply dwarfing a plant. The shaping—whether done by bending and wiring or by trimming—is strictly the artist's option.

Any plant can be made into a bonsai. Trees, flowers, grasses, and fruits can all be dwarfed, but coniferous evergreens are probably the most popular of all plants for bonsai—maybe because the average person inevitably finds a little tree more interesting than a little dandelion.

Bonsais are sold everywhere these days—they're very "in" in the retail plant business—but they're also very expensive. Aside from the personal rewards of creating your own beautiful and exotic plant, the potential savings may be reason enough for you to try make your own.

Although I do know how to make a bonsai, I thought I'd turn to Patti Lee (of New York City and Hawaii), America's foremost authority on this subject, for the "compleat" story. Patti's bonsais (and other plants) have won ribbons and trophies at every major flower-and-plant show in America, and what follows is her advice as to how to make your own bonsai.

STARTING WITH THE RIGHT PLANT

Since you're going to be growing your bonsai indoors, start by picking a plant that does not need a hard, cold winter dormancy to survive. This includes virtually any tropical plant, along with certain conifers.

How large or small or how young or old the plant you should choose is strictly up to you. You can begin with a very small, very young plant, or a larger, more established plant. A plant that's two or three years old is probably best, since it's already had a chance to adapt to growing in a container. Since it's very difficult to judge the age of a plant unless you've grown it from seed yourself, you might as well just pick a plant you like as far as size, shape, and variety are concerned.

If you can find a little plant that's potbound—overgrown and stunted in too small a pot—all the better. You're liable to find such treasures if you look in the back of large nurseries or where the nurseryman stows his "junk" plants. You may find a perfect candidate for bonsai back there—something gnarled and neglected and overgrown and potbound. These plants are perfect for bonsai, but difficult to sell, so you're likely to get it for a very good price.

Patti suggests the Hinoki cypress (*Chamaecyparis obtusa*) as the most practical plant for a starter bonsai. This plant grows very well indoors in any climate and has the evergreen look that most beginners prefer.

Pick a cypress—or whatever other plant you choose—with some semblance of a trunk and a good, strong lower branch about one-third of the way up.

GETTING BACK TO YOUR ROOTS

The rules for turning whatever plant you pick into a bonsai are the same.

The first step is to take the plant out of its pot and remove the dirt from its roots with a chopstick or a pencil. *(Ill. 21)*

You should only do this in late winter or early spring—when the plant is just coming out of dormancy and new growth is just starting, so that it will be less of a shock to the plant's root system.

Carefully untangle the roots and remove the soil from around the root ball—but leave some soil around the inner root ball itself. This is important. Although some books say to wash all the soil off the root system, Ms. Lee insists this is wrong, wrong, wrong, and will severely diminish the plant's chances of surviving.

Once you've untangled the roots with your chopstick and carefully brushed away all of the soil except that directly around the innermost root ball, take a

Ill. 21 *Ill. 22*

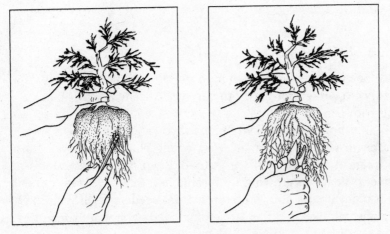

scissors and, snipping all around the plant (not just around the bottom), cut away about one-third of the root mass. *(Ill. 22)*

Now set the plant in a shallow bonsai pot—which can be purchased in most nurseries and garden centers, or better yet in a store that specializes in bonsai.

Press the plant down into the pot—adding potting mix if necessary. In most cases the plant will be slightly mounded, or raised above the top of the pot. This condition will last for about a year, after which the plant will begin to sink slowly until the soil is a tiny bit below the edge of the pot. It usually takes several growing seasons before you'll get the plant to conform perfectly to the pot. In a perfectly proportioned bonsai, the height of the pot would be no more than the width of the trunk of the plant. *(Ill. 23)*

You should only wire the plant if you want to alter the angle or direction of a branch or the trunk. If you decide you want to make a drastic change in the plant's shape, wait until the plant is well established—after about six months. Bend the trunk or branch to the desired angle and wrap it with copper wire so that it will hold its position. Depending upon the plant and the effect you want, it often takes years and years of training before you can take the wire off the plant.

Ms. Lee prefers to shape her bonsais by trimming—a process much like shaping a hedge. *(Ill. 24)* By constantly clipping and pruning the foliage you can create any shape you want. This method is more time-consuming than wiring, but Ms. Lee feels that in the long run it's better for the plant. You'll have to continue this trimming process for the life of your bonsai—which can be over 100 years.

It's this trimming and pruning that determines the size of your bonsai and makes it look different from other plants. The difference is *not* due to the root trimming, which isn't needed after the initial trim. You only trim the roots so that the plant can be contained in its small, shallow dish.

Ill. 23

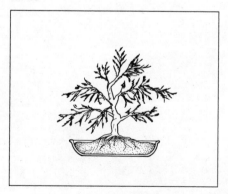

Ill. 24

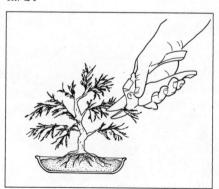

CARING FOR YOUR BONSAI

Once you've finished making your bonsai, care for it just as you would the same species and variety if it were regularly potted. As Ms. Lee points out, "basically, it's just a plant."

However, you should carefully trim the foliage back once a month or so, and feed the plant much less than usual—only about once every six weeks during the growing season. If there's one special key to bonsai care it's to be sure that you water *more* frequently than usual—the plant's smaller, shallower root-system needs more frequent watering.

Your Hinoki cypress, for example, needs bright sunlight, watering when the top of the soil dries out, and medium humidity—you should spray it at least once a day.

LEARNING MORE ABOUT BONSAI

There are lots of books about bonsai. Most include photographs, or at least elaborate illustrations, that can help you make any of the classic bonsai styles: Kabu-mono—a pot containing a single plant with any number of stems; Chokkan—a single tree; Shakan—a slanting form that imitates a tree growing at right angles to a mountain slope, and many more.

But Ms. Lee's feeling—and I wholeheartedly agree—is that, while a book can be helpful, if you really want to get involved in making your own bonsais you should seek out someone who deals specifically in these beautiful living sculptures and ask for a hands-on lesson or demonstration. In fact, if you live in a major city, bonsai classes are probably available—and highly recommended.

The rewards of doing it yourself are tremendous—and whatever you pay for the lessons will soon seem cheap compared to what you'd pay to buy the ready-made plants.

EPILOGUE

Well, there you have it. You've been introduced to all the most rewarding, exotic, glamorous, sophisticated, beautiful, indoor plants that can be grown without a greenhouse. I repeat—successfully cultivating these plants will give you some of the most fulfilling experiences you'll ever have. I promise.

And, as I told you fifteen years ago, Mr. Mother Earth would never tell a little green lie.

GLOSSARY

Aerial Root: Some plants take in moisture and nutrients through roots which grow above the ground—out from the stem of the plant. These aerial roots can remain growing freely, or you can plant them in soil.

Annual: A plant that grows from seed to maturity in a single year. It is generally thrown away after its blooming season.

Biennial: A plant that grows from seed to maturity in two years, flowering and seeding the second year.

Bonsai: The Japanese art of creating and cultivating dwarf trees. This Japanese term (meaning "planted in a tray") refers both to the dwarfed plant and to the art of creating that plant.

Bract: A modified leaf, often brightly colored, appearing on the stalk between the flower and the normal leaves on plants with relatively insignificant flowers. The bright red foliage of the poinsettia is technically a bract.

Bulb: An underground bud that can develop roots and produce leaves and flowers. The bulb stores food during the plant's dormant period. Examples of plants that you can grow from bulbs include tulips and daffodils.

Corm: Similar to a bulb, a corm is a rounded, thickened, underground stem base covered with a thin papery skin. A bud at the top of the corm produces both roots and shoots. Crocus plants are grown from corms.

Crown: The central part of the plant, just below the soil, where the stem and root join.

Cultivar: A plant species or variety that has been deliberately bred for cultivation.

Dormancy: A seasonal period, usually during the winter, when a plant's growth stops or slows down.

Dry Well: A tray filled with pebbles and water on which plants sit. The water evaporates, providing the extra humidity that many plants need to grow indoors.

Epiphyte: A plant, such as an orchid or Spanish moss, which takes its water and essential nutrients from the air. In nature, epiphytes often grown on other plants, but unlike parasitic plants use the other plants only for support.

Family: A group of plant species which are related in a botanical sense, but are not always similar in appearance. Also known as a genus.

Frond: A botanical term used to describe the long, branching leaves of certain ferns. The term is also applied to describe palm leaves.

Humus: Decomposed organic matter often added to potting mix. The organic portion of soil derived form decomposed animal or plant matter.

Loam: Soil containing a mixture of humus, clay, and sand.

Lobe: The center portion of the leaf or petal.

Mildew: A white furry fungus that can appear on unhealthy plants. Mildew is caused by too much dampness and not enough air.

Node: A joint where leaves or buds emerge from the stem.

Offset (Also, *Offshoot*): A plantlet, or smaller version of the full-grown plant, which grows from the plant's base and can be used to propagate a new plant.

Perennial: A plant that lives for three or more growing seasons and blooms year after year.

Perlite: A porous volcanic rock, usually greyish in color, which is often mixed with other soils or potting mix to increase soil drainage.

Pinnate: Resembling a feather, such as the leaves of a palm or a fern frond.

Propagation: Increasing plants by means of stem cuttings, leaf cuttings, air layering, seeds, or division.

Rhizome: A thick stem, generally growing horizontally underground or at the surface of the soil, with buds, leaves, and roots similar to bulbs, corms, and tubers.

Shrub: A woody-stemmed plant with no significant main trunk.

Spathe: A leaflike structure which encases a flower. The peace lily is a good example of a plant with a prominent spathe.

Standard: A shrub, or woody-stemmed plant, that has been trained and pruned to have a long, slender, single trunk and bushy top. Some standards reach a height of up to three feet.

Stolon: A long-rooting runner, such as on spider plants or strawberry begonias, from which new plants grow.

Stomata: The pores, or breathing cells, of the leaves.

Succulent: A flesh-leafed member of the cactus family which can store moisture in its leaves and stems for extended periods of time. The jade plant is probably the best-known succulent.

Systemic: An insecticide put directly into the soil of an infested plant.

Topiaries: Topiaries are plants and shrubs which have been trained to grow in two- and three-dimensional shapes by binding their stems and branches to wire frames and pruning them carefully.

Transpiration: The process which gives off moisture through the stomata.

Tuber: An underground stem with eyes or buds that can produce shoots that develop into upright stems. The tuberous begonia and cyclamen are good examples of plants that grow from tubers.

Variegated: Multicolored.

Variety: A subdivision of a species.

Vermiculite: A water-retentive mineral most often used as a growing medium for seeds, cuttings and seedlings.

PLANT LISTS

Choosing the right plant for you—one that will thrive on the environment and the care you can provide—is one of the most important parts of caring for these most-rewarding plants.

The lists that follow can help you discover that perfect plant for you. If you're choosing a gift for someone else, remember that any plant makes a great gift—as long as it is compatible with the recipient and the conditions in their home (or office), is delivered healthy, and comes with specific instructions for proper care.

Flowering Plants (cont.)

Gardenia 81
Geranium 82
Gloxinia 83
Goldfish plant 85
Heliotrope 89
Hibiscus *or* Chinese hibiscus 90
Hyacinth 91
Jasmine 96
Kafir lily 97
Lipstick plant 99
Orchid 111
Snow rose 129

Hanging Plants

Arrowhead plant 33
Asparagus fern 35
Baby's tears 38
Boston fern 44
Burro's tail *or* Donkey's tail 46
Coleus 58
Devil's ivy *or* Pothus 65
English ivy 70
Fuchsia 80
Goldfish plant 85
Grape ivy 86
Jasmine 96
Lipstick plant 99
Pigglyback plant 117
Purple velvet 122
Purple waffle plant 123
Rabbit's-foot fern 124
Shrimp plant 128
Spider plant 131
String-of-hearts *or* Rosary vine 134
String-of-pearls 135
Swedish ivy 136
Wandering Jew 141
Wax plant *or* Hindu rope plant 142

Plants for Kids

Cast-iron plant *or* Aspidistra 53
Devil's ivy *or* Pothus 65
Earth star 69
Living rocks 100
Miracle leaf plant 104
Pineapple 118
Prayer plant 121
Sensitive plant *or* Action plant 127
Spanish moss 130
Venus flytrap 140

Plants for Low Light

Arrowhead plant 33
Artillery plant 34
Baby's tears 38
Button fern 48
Cast-iron plant *or* Aspidistra 53
Chinese evergreen 55
Corn plant 59
Devil's ivy *or* Pothos 65
Irish moss *or* Spike moss 94
Kentia palm 98
Maidenhair fern 101
Neanthe bella palm *or* Dwarf
   palm 108
Sensitive plant *or* Action plant 127
Staghorn fern 132
Swiss cheese plant 137

INDEX